WORLD HERITAGE SITES IN SWEDEN

Leif Anker

Gunilla Litzell

Bengt A Lundberg

The Swedish Institute

The National Heritage Board

This book is the English version of *Världsarv i Sverige* (The National Heritage Board, 2002). It is published by The National Heritage Board and the Swedish Institute.

Text:
Leif Anker (chapters 3, 4, 5, 6, 7, 8, 11 and 12 in the original, adapted from the book *Our Nordic Heritage: World Heritage Sites in the Nordic Countries*/ Leif Anker, Ingalill Snitt, 1997)
Gunilla Litzell (chapters 1, 2, 9 and 10 in the original)

The authors alone are responsible for the opinions expressed in this book.

Photo:
Bengt A Lundberg, RAÄ,
except on pages:
6 Metria/Satellus, Lantmäteriet
51 (right) *Gabriel Hildebrand*, RAÄ
91, 92-93, 94 and 97 *Jan Norrman*, RAÄ
96 and 98 *Mats Frii*
103 *Leif Forslund*, Foto Dalmas
112, 113 and 143 (below) *Kjell Ljungström*
116 (below) and 118 (above) *Lars Guva*
130 *Gunnel Friberg*

Design:
Klas Danielsson

Editor:
Ulla von Schultz

Translation:
Roger Tanner

© 2002 The National Heritage Board
and the Swedish Institute
1:1

Printed in Sweden by Edita, Västra Aros 2002

ISBN 91-7209-255-6 (hard cover – The National Heritage Board)
ISBN 91-520-0707-3 (soft cover – The Swedish Institute)

Contents

A World Heritage site is a place, a building, a monument or a natural feature of outstanding universal value from the point of view of history or natural science. In order to make this vital natural and cultural heritage identifiable and protectable, UNESCO took the initiative in framing the 1972 Convention Concerning the Protection of the World Cultural and Natural Heritage. This has attracted enormous interest ever since, with more than 160 countries acceding. Sweden became a signatory in 1985.

How are World Heritage sites identified and how can one be sure that the choice made in a particular country represents the outstanding value called for?

A number of criteria which have to be met offer useful guidance for the selection process, e.g. the stipulation of authenticity.

Usually World Heritage sites are to be found among places of national importance – "national interest" sites, historic buildings and national parks. To determine their international importance, we have to look around us in the world at large for similar places and penomena, analysing similarities and differences.

Sweden and the other Nordic countries have resolved this problem by co-operating in the selection process. As a result, archaeological remains, Nordic building traditions, buildings painted with Falun red paint ("Swedish Red"), unique areas of natural scenery, isostatic uplift phenomena, Sami culture, industrial buildings and buildings of the 20th century have come to occupy the forefront.

It is an honour for any nation to have part of its cultural heritage or one of its natural phenomena added to the UNESCO World Heritage List. The fact of a small country like Sweden being represented by twelve items gives us cause for both pride and humility, demonstrating as it does the importance attached, not only by ourselves but also by the rest of the world, to our abundant cultural and natural history.

Needless to say, this also means a great deal to the communities and regions with World Heritage sites in their vicinity. It gives them a symbol to highlight and to rally round, and, with places of natural and cultural interest attracting more and more visitors, it provides an important boost for the local economy.

At the same time as the designation of a World Heritage site is an honour, it also implies obligations. We pledge ourselves to manage the place, building or site and to take such good care of it that it will remain intact for future generations. The National Heritage Board and the Swedish Environmental Protection Agency have been tasked with supervising the discharge of that responsibility, but in the everyday run of things it is shared by all citizens.

Let us now begin our journey in time and space. From the era when the ice cap began to give way to what is now the High Coast, to the harmony and tranquillity of the 20th century Woodland Cemetery. From the naval port of Karlskrona in the south to the huge expanses of Lapland in the north, from the prehistoric rock carvings of Tanum in the west to the Hanseatic town of Visby in the east.

On behalf of the National Heritage Board

Erik Wegræus, Director-General

On behalf of the Swedish
Environmental Protection Agency

Lars-Erik Liljelund, Director-General

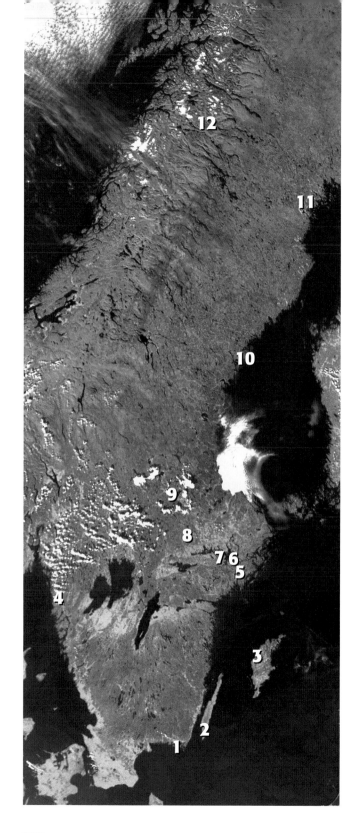

Sweden's Twelve World Heritage Sites

1 The Naval Port of Karlskrona
2 The Agricultural Landscape of Southern Öland
3 The Hanseatic Town of Visby
4 The Rock Carvings in Tanum
5 Skogskyrkogården – The Woodland Cemetery
6 The Royal Domain of Drottningholm
7 Birka and Hovgården
8 The Engelsberg Ironworks
9 The Mining Area of the Great Copper Mountain in Falun
10 Höga Kusten – The High Coast
11 Gammelstad Church Town, Luleå
12 Laponia

The Naval Port
of Karlskrona

For over three centuries, most things in and about Karlskrona have centred round the naval dockyard, the harbour and the defence works. This unique industrial setting has witnessed a continuous evolution of naval architecture and shipbuilding, from the "High Seas Fleet" of Karl XI, which ruled the waves of the 17th century Baltic, right down to our own time and the sophisticated stealth vessels emerging from the shipbuilding company Karlskronavarvet.

Sweden during the second half of the 17th century was one of the great powers of Europe. Although it was a small, remote country, poor and sparsely populated, the very mention of its army was enough to make all the kings and emperors of Europe shift uneasily. Sweden had nearly achieved the great dream of all the Baltic countries – *Dominium Maris Baltici*, mastery of the Baltic Sea. Its navy, therefore, was no less important than its army, and King Karl XI had great plans. In 1679 he decreed the establishment of a new base, and a year later the site was appointed – Trossö, in what is now the Karlskrona Archipelago.

This was chosen partly as being within easy reach of Sweden's possessions across the Baltic, including Stralsund and Riga, two of the principal cities of the realm.

The naval base was to be provided with a dockyard, storage buildings, barracks, offices for the Admiralty College – a new town was to be quickly set in motion, complete with labourers, craftsmen and sailors. The means adopted to this end was uncommonly brutal. The neighbouring town of Ronneby was robbed of its charter and its population ordered to move to Karlskrona. This act of tyranny was resolved on from the very outset, inscribed in the new town's charter.

A famous 17th century Swede, Erik Dahlbergh, was commissioned by the King to plan and design the new community. Only two years later, more than 2,000 men were busy on the site. During the following 150 years, some of Sweden's most eminent architects – Nicodemus Tessin the Elder and Younger, Carl August Ehrensvärd and Olof Tempelman, in addition to Dahlbergh himself – worked to create a city of international standing.

The city takes shape

A traveller in 1753 wrote in his diary: "Carlscrone is built on nothing but rock, the streets going up and down it,

Page 7: The Enlistment and Model Hall building from 1784 was designed by Fredric Henric af Chapman. The columned façade forms part of an enfilade consisting of several buildings. Above: The old mast crane is a closed stone tower, completed in 1806. It took 96 men to turn the windlass.

so one has to beware of falling and breaking an arm or a leg." It was not until the mid-19th century that work began on paving Stortorget ("Main Square"), and it was only completed towards the end of the century.

Amiralitetsgatan ("Admiralty Street") was laid out right across the island. Immediately to the south of it,

living quarters were built for senior officers – large, beautiful houses on generous plots of ground. Next came the dockyard. Along the eastern shore, large warehouses and living quarters were built for civilian traders. Humble cottages for dockyard workers were built on Västerudd ("West Point") and Björkholmen ("Birch Island").

Main Square was the hub of the city, dominated by the three monumental official buildings: The Courthouse, the Fredrik Church and Trefaldighetskyrkan (Trinity Church). With the opening, in 1798, of the Courthouse, designed probably by Thure Wennberg, Main Square was considered complete. The two churches, designed by Nicodemus Tessin the Younger, rank among the foremost monuments of the classical Roman Baroque in Sweden. Fredrik Church was built between 1720 and 1758, and Trinity Church (originally known, after its congregation, as the German Church) was built between 1697 and 1749. The oldest church of all, the Admiralty Church of Ulrica Pia, was built in 1685 – of timber, because it was needed in a hurry.

The history of Karlskrona is very much the history of its naval port and fortifications. The dockside area has many imposing and remarkable buildings. With activities going on here ever since the city was founded,

Left: The Fredrik Church and statue of Karl XI in Main Square. The north tower has two small bells, one of them bearing Gustav III's monogram. A larger bell hangs in the south tower. The two smaller ones had to be recast after the fire which swept the town in 1790, while the larger one escaped undamaged.
Above: The Courthouse in Main Square, here seen from Trinity Church, has been several times extended.
Below: Shoring from the five-finger docks of Trossö.

Left: The arsenal in the foreground and, behind it, the af Trolle Battalion, within the barrack perimeter.
Middle: The fortified tower on Godnatt Skerry was built in 1863 and decommissioned seven years later. In 1870 it was converted into a manned navigation light for the shipping lane.
Right: The Aurora Bastion was named after the Goddess of the Dawn in Roman mythology, located as it is at the far eastern end of the naval base.

each new century has contributed new buildings. In 1716, for example, Charles XII decreed the building of an English-style dry dock. The inventor Christopher Polhem was tasked with solving the problem of how to drain it. Here, unlike England, no help was forthcoming from tides. Polhem designed a bucket chain with 270 men working in three shifts for up to four days to empty the dock of water. The Naval Model Chamber was established by King Adolf Fredrik in 1752. At that time models were made of every ship built and put on display in the Enlistment and Model Hall building. In 1778 Carl August Ehrensvärd designed Inventariekammare I (Inventory Chamber I), popularly known as the Silver House after Gustav III had sarcastically enquired whether it was being

built of silver instead of stone and mortar. This building is divided into four sections in which the same number of ships could deposit their equipment for winter storage.

The fortifications

The Trossö installations, the marine authorities, the barracks, the dockyard and the naval port, were to be defended by a line of fortifications on islands and skerries outside the city. Furthest out, at Aspösund, the inlet to the Inner Archipelago was defended by Drottningskär Fort and Kungsholm Fortress.

Nearer to the base, fortified towers were eventually built on Kurrholmen and on Godnatt ("Good Night") Skerry. That was in the mid-19th century, but within a few years the towers were obsolete. The eastern side of Trossö was defended by extensive fortifications on Koholmen ("Cow Island") and a gun tower on Mjölnareholmen ("Miller's Island"). From there, in wintertime, the naval base could be guarded against an assault over the ice.

Several small islands, such as Björkholmen, Lindholmen and Söderstjärna, were allotted functions to do with

Left: The construction of the Wasa Shed at the beginning of the 1760s enabled shipbuilding to continue all the year round, whatever the weather. The shed remained in use for that purpose until about 1900.

Right: The Rope-Walk from the 1690s is the most outstanding building from the dockyard's earliest history. A 300-metre-long wooden walk extends between two stone abutments.

the central base. They also became physically united, after the straits between them had been filled in. This area includes several quite unique buildings, such as Repslagarbanan ("the Rope-Walk") and Wasaskjulet ("the Wasa Shed") on Lindholmen. Workshops and provision stores were built on Stumholmen, which is nearest Trossö. This island also has a very unusual building from the end of the 18th century, known as Slup- och barkassskjulet ("the Sloop and Longboat Shed"). The main inlet to the Inner Archipelago, between Aspö and Tjurkö, is the weakest point in the defensive shield round Trossö, because Kungsdjupet (nowadays called Aspösund) is nearly one-and-a-half kilometres across.

Kungsholm Fortress was a good deal bigger than Drottningskär Fort, where work already started in 1680 to build a donjon as big as the skerry itself. A donjon is a massive stone building of several storeys with covered positions for the fortress artillery. All through the 18th century and some way into the 19th, this remained the most important defensive installation of all.

Kungsholm Fortress was originally relatively simple and a good deal less strong than the structure on the other side of Aspösund. During the 1830s it was radically altered, enlarged and modernised. Although it was garrisoned continuously for over 320 years, it never fired a shot in anger.

Kungsholm Fortress had an armament of 400 guns and a garrison of between 1,100 and 1,200. It has been placed on a war footing three times in the past 150 years: during the Crimean War and during both world wars. It was also the headquarters of the submarine hunts of the 1980s.

One very special feature of Kungsholmen is its circular sloop harbour. The oldest surviving building on Kungsholmen is Stora Kruthuset ("the Great Powder Magazine"), completed in 1736.

In addition to military personnel, the inmates of the fort also included convicts sentenced to hard labour. Theirs was a hard life indeed. Their working day could start at 4 in the morning, continuing until 8 at night. Floggings were not uncommon, and there were also executions. The officers and their families had a pleasant life of it.

Previous spread: At its strongest, the Drottningskär Fort had a garrison of 250 and an armament of 77 guns and ten mortars.
Left: View from the entrance to Skärva Manor.
Below: The main building at Skärva with its Doric portico.
Next page: The arcade beneath the Model Hall in the Enlistment and Model Hall building.

The officers' wives were allowed to employ sailors as domestic servants. Senta Centervall, whose father commanded the Carlskrona Artillery Corps at the end of the 19th century, wrote: "They could be employed for any tasks about the home. They were invaluable, modest, hard-working and astonishingly reliable in the matter of looking after the children." The last family to have lived here all the year round moved out of the fort in 1959. Kungsholmen has always been an important workplace, and remains so today.

The hinterland

In the country round about Karlskrona, officers and wealthy citizens built summer retreats for themselves. Eventually the city acquired a whole girdle of fine manor-ial residences, often complete with working farms. These are represented on the World Heritage List by Skärva, the country residence of Admiral of the Dockyard Fredric Henric af Chapman. Skärva Manor was built in 1785-86, and af Chapman designed it himself. The main building is a timbered cottage. Both its craftsmanship and the structural solutions proclaim the whole manor as the work of experienced ship's carpenters. An English-style park was landscaped round the main building, with a Temple of Diana and a Gothic Tower as eye-catchers.

Water supply was a major problem in Karlskrona right from the beginning. There simply wasn't enough fresh water for the whole population. A dam and waterworks were therefore constructed on the lowest fall of the Lyckeby River already in the 1710s, and this remains the city's source of water supply. Lyckeby was important in other ways too. Among other things, it had a Crown mill which kept two large Crown bakeries supplied with flour.

The city's military soul has gradually turned civilian. The well-preserved military installations have acquired a new significance, as an example of a well-planned European naval base.

THE NAVAL PORT OF KARLSKRONA

The Agricultural Landscape of Southern Öland

Man has been leaving his mark on Öland for at least four thousand years. Nature has been setting limits to human enterprise for the same length of time. This process of interaction has resulted in the unique natural and man-made environment which we call the agricultural landscape of Southern Öland.

The whole of the Baltic island of Öland was a royal hunting park from 1569, when Johan III introduced "Regalia Right". This greatly transformed the living conditions of the permanent population. Farmers were no longer permitted even to break off branches from trees or gather leaves, but they were at least allowed to graze their livestock in the outfields. The King's game animals were allowed to roam freely, and the farmers, being forbidden to bear arms, were unable to defend their fields. Wild boar were the paramount pest. This royal hunting park and its attendant regulations were not abolished until 1801.

Today the new and old live side by side – modern detached houses and medieval linear villages, industries and

prehistoric forts, modern farming and Iron Age burials. Windmills and stonewalls are the best-known features of the Öland landscape. It is less well known that practically all the brown beans eaten in Sweden are grown on this island.

In a manner of speaking, the Öland landscape within the World Heritage site is candy-striped. In the southwest we have the Mörbylånga valley, containing the best farmland in Öland. On the inside of that is Västra Landborgen, a raised cliff between 20 and 40 metres high. In the middle of Southern Öland is Stora Alvaret, a peculiar mosaic of gravel outcrops, limestone pan and grasslands. To the east of this are coastlands and coastal meadows, giving way to a "rim" of cultivable land. Furthest east are the raised beaches of Östra Landborgen, rising from a few metres to about 13 metres above sea level. A cross-section of the island also reveals a slope from west to east.

Stora Alvaret

Stora Alvaret is a unique habitat. Limestone pan of this kind occurs in only a few places on earth, and Öland's is the most extensive of them all, 260 km². The precondition for this type of formation is a calcareous bedrock with a very thin overburden which is alternately subjected to extreme drought and inundation. The present-day landscape has come about through the combination bedrock, climate and livestock grazing. If it were not for constant grazing, this remarkable place would become overgrown.

Species grow here which are normally to be found only in the south of Europe, the mountain region or Siberia, and there are also plants here – the white or Öland rock-rose, and the *Artemisia laciniata* species of wormwood – which occur nowhere else in the world.

Alvar dry grasslands occur on ridges with slightly deeper overburden, while the declivities consist of calcareous moist grasslands. Both these types of grassland depend on grazing livestock to keep them from becoming overgrown with trees and bushes. Where the soil is very thin and also calcareous, sheep's fescue and rock-rose heaths occur. This landscape resembles the tundra which extended all over northern Europe after the last glacial. The limestone bedrock alvar consists almost entirely of bare limestone slabs where mainly mosses and lichens

Page 21: This view of horses at pasture near Gettlinge sums up the very essence of Öland – the open landscape, stone walls and the riot of flowers.
Top left: Adam-and-Eve, one of Öland's many orchids.
Left: Orminge Rör has been grazing land for many generations. The partly denuded bushes are Öland shrubby cinquefoil. Ottenby Nature Reserve and the Långe Jan lighthouse on the southern tip of Öland are visible in the background.

can survive. The karst alvar has deep fissures in its soil-free limestone slabs. The bottoms of these fissures are favourable habitats for species which normally belong to a different environment. There are *vät* formations and alvar lakes scattered here and there. *Vät* is the name for water-filled declivities which dry out in summer.

The first dated anthropogenic remains on the alvar are passage graves from the Neolithic. The Iron Age is represented by house foundations and small burial grounds. The entire alvar is traversed by a network – 380 km long altogether – of holloways which have been hollowed into the ground surface by prolonged use.

The coastlands and coastal meadows

"Coastlands" is the name of the flat area near the Baltic coast, parallel to the cultivated soil. For millennia these lands have been grazed by livestock; the east coast was already colonised by cattle-herding islanders during the Iron Age. Because the coastlands have never been cultivated, settlement remains are clearly discernible – oblong hall-houses with stone walls and stone boundaries marking drovers' paths, milking pens and enclosures. Right down to the Second World War, dairy cows grazed on the coastlands and were milked on the spot, as had been the practice for thousands of years.

These lands have never been treated with artificial fertiliser, hence their tremendous biodiversity. In addition they include the most important resting habitats in northern Europe for all the Arctic migrant birds stopping off here. The coastlands are also a nesting ground for seabirds and waders depending on open, grazed country.

The coastal meadows are lands close to the shoreline where farmers have been able to cut hay for winter fodder.

Above: This old gravel road can be followed straight across the coastlands at Gräsgård in the municipality of Mörbylånga.
Left: Öland has Sweden's greatest diversity of species of all the provinces of Sweden, in relation to area.
Right: Gettlinge burial ground. The prow of the ship-setting has cup-marks at the top. Scholars have yet to deduce their function.

These meadows were fenced in, to exclude grazing live-stock, and were therefore counted among the in-fields – the common pasture of the village. The coastlands, on the other hand, belonged to the outfields, and as such were only used as pasture for free-ranging livestock.

Man and the agricultural landscape

The first humans came to Öland roughly eight thousand years ago. They were hunter-gatherers and settled along the coasts. At the Alby settlement archaeologists have found traces of Stone Age huts. This place was inhabited for two thousand years, until about 4000 BC.

It was during the Neolithic that people in Öland began tilling the soil and herding cattle, during the period known as the Agrarian Stone Age. The earliest passage graves are from the end of this period, e.g. at Resmo, which shows that settlements were permanent. The division of labour still prevailing today, with arable farming predominating on the western side and livestock farming on the eastern side, was established already then.

During the two millennia preceding the Christian era, the people of southern Öland probably had a good life, in a warm and pleasant climate and with enough food for everyone.

Living conditions changed in many ways at the beginning of the Christian era. Farmers lived in small villages where they had established arable fields and went in for dairy farming on a considerable scale. Times had grown more turbulent. The great prehistoric forts were now in use, though they did not become permanently inhabited until later. Today we know of five prehistoric forts within the World Heritage site – Sandby, Bårby, Triberga, Träby and Eketorp. These forts were really fortified villages where the local farmsteads had joined forces for the protection of people and property.

Land subdivision and linear villages

The present-day subdivision of land evolved in the 12th century and the three centuries that followed it, complete with village tofts, in-fields and outfields. The cultivated land – in-fields – was enclosed and the outfields were used as pasture. The large village toft was divided up between the farmsteads, and the typical Öland linear village took shape.

In a linear village, all holdings are lined up alongside the village street. The farmstead lots vary in width, ac-

Previous spread: In this pastoral setting at Enetri time seems to have stood still. Cattle sheds and outbuildings of rough limestone are gently embraced by lush greenery.
Top left: At Lilla Frö one can peep in through this gateway to a farmyard surrounded by a traditional Geatish homestead.
Bottom left: Lilla Frö is a typical Öland linear village.
Above: Coastlands at Hulterstad.

cording to how large a share of the village's communal production the owner was entitled to. The commonest type of farmstead in the linear villages of Öland is the so-called Geatish farmstead. The rectangular plot is surrounded by buildings, and dwelling house and outbuildings – "dwelling yard" and "cattle yard" – are separated by a wall or fence, with the outbuildings next to the street. From the village street the farmstead is entered by a gateway. Linear villages were common everywhere in eastern Sweden and in northern Europe during medieval times, but today they survive almost exclusively in southern Öland.

Many stone churches were built on the island in the 12th century, the oldest being those of Hulterstad and Resmo. Stone churches at this time were parochial fortresses. Öland needed protection for its wealth and population when times were troubled. The character of these buildings remained unaltered until the 19th century, when the large, single-aisled church superseded the defensive church, for the simple reason that the older churches could no longer accommodate all the parishioners.

When the royal hunting privileges were abolished in 1801, the outfields were parcelled out among the villages,

which saw to it that each farmer received his rightful share. This distribution of the outfields was completed in 1819, and it was at this time that the windmills came into being. Many farmers wanted to have their own mills on their own land: 200 years ago the windmill was something of a status symbol. In the mid-19th century Öland had almost 2,000 of them. Today 350 remain – 62 of them within the World Heritage site.

The acreage under the plough more than tripled when land distribution reforms were carried out. From the mid-19th century and for roughly a hundred years thereafter, stone walls were constructed, marking the boundaries between holdings. But the walls separating village in-fields from outfields date from the Middle Ages.

Despite all this breaking of new land, the island had increasing difficulty in supporting its growing population. Legislation passed following the land distribution reforms laid down that farmsteads could not be parti-

The coastal meadows at Gräsgård have supplied genera-tions of Öland farmers with forage for their livestock.

tioned more than twice, and sometimes this could have tragic consequences. If there were three or more children in a family, the farmstead would be inherited by the two eldest. The younger ones would be "left over" and would have to make a living as best they could, most often as servant maids and farmhands. Many were marginalised altogether and reduced to begging, while others sought salvation by emigrating. One-third of Öland's population emigrated between 1880 and 1930.

But in spite of the trend in favour of larger farming units, and the rural depopulation by which the whole of Sweden has been affected, Öland's arable acreage has not changed. The man-made landscape looks much the same as it has done for thousands of years. It is as a living landscape that southern Öland retains its unique qualities.

The Hanseatic Town of Visby

Visby in the 13th century was a bustle of activity. In those days, the town's harbour occupied what is now Almedalen park. A town and its encircling wall sprang up in less than a hundred years. Stone and lime for mortar were quarried from the cliffs surrounding the town. Packhouses, quays, the town wall, churches and monasteries were all built in an amazingly short period of time.

Visby lies halfway down the long west coast of Gotland. Today it is the municipality's "central locality", with a population of some 20,000. The inner city is girt about by the well-preserved town wall. Inside the wall, massive ruined churches and solid stone houses testify to the city's heyday in the 13th century, when it was the nodal point of Baltic trade and one of the most important and wealthiest cities in northern Europe.

Gotland was already an important trading centre in prehistoric times. Copious archaeological finds from the

Migration and Merovingian periods (400-700 AD) illustrate trade links extending along the Baltic coasts, from Denmark in the west to Russia in the east. A succession of rune stones from the 11th century tell of yeomen-merchants from Gotland – "yeoman adventurers" – who died in foreign places.

Gotland society was based on relatively equal, landed peasants with a "common law" and a separate judicial system. Much of their living came from transit trade. Hides and wax from Russia and Finland were shipped westwards and exchanged for textiles and luxury goods. Swedish iron was forged into weapons and implements and dispatched eastwards.

Gutasagan, written down in about 1220, relates that the Gotlanders placed themselves under the protection of the King of the Svear in present-day Sweden, paying an annual tax of 12 kilos of silver, equalling 10 grams each for the island's 1,200 homesteads. But Gotland retained its autonomy, tax exemption and exemption from the *ledung* naval levy.

Visby's earliest history

Nobody knows when Visby was founded. A Stone Age settlement has been found in the city, but otherwise – unlike the rest of Gotland – Visby shows few traces of extensive settlement or agriculture from prehistoric times. *Gutasagan* tells of Botair, who built a church at Vi, presumably where the ruined churches of St Per and St Hans now stand. No date is given for this event, but it is pre-

Previous page: View from the parapet of the north wall.
Left: The crowstep gable of the old pharmacy in Strandgatan. Originally a 13th century packhouse and one of the best-preserved medieval buildings in Visby.

sumed to have occurred in the first half of the 11th century. According to *Gutasagan*, Gotland was converted to Christianity by St Olof, King of Norway.

It is assumed that Vi – the future Visby – started off as an anchorage for the yeomen adventurers who, in Viking times, only lived here at a certain time of the year. A sandbank created a natural, sheltered harbour on the otherwise exposed west coast of Gotland. At the water's edge, there are terraced limestone cliffs. Remains of timber houses from the Viking era, two or three metres below the present-day ground level, have been dated to just before AD 1000. The shoreline at that time followed roughly the course of present-day Strandgatan. The settlement fanned out in parallel lines from the shore, up between present-day Hästgatan in the south and Skogränd in the north. Huts were built in pairs, their fronts overlooking what are now Mellangatan and St Hansgatan. Similar patterns of settlement – houses in pairs, their ends facing a waterfront or quayside and with small lanes between them – occur in other towns later on in the medieval period, e.g. at Bryggen in Bergen. The oldest part of Visby's city centre with a rectilinear pattern of settlement stand out from the otherwise more irregular street configuration of the town, with its variously sized plots.

From agrarian trade to Hanseatic town

Visby grew in commercial importance during the 12th century, when trade passed from the yeomen adventurers to specialised merchants. At the same time the permanent population grew and the town

From top: Window with fine shutters, Norra Murgatan.
Window tracery in the ruined church of St Nicolaus. Decorated doorway in Klintgatan.
Part of a picture-stone in St Gertrud's Gränd.
Restrained architecture, complete with panelled doors. House in Kilgränd from 1765.
The Visby Botanical Gardens were founded in 1856 by the Society of Bathing Friends.

expanded. A new parish church, St Clemens, was built in the northern part of the town. Russians and Germans came to Visby, only for the summer season to begin with. In the 1130s the merchants of Gotland were granted trading privileges by the German Emperor Lothair, and in 1161 Gotland signed a commercial treaty with the newly established town of Lübeck. That treaty opened up trading routes between the Gotlanders and the Germans. In addition, Visby merchants sailed to the countries bordering on the North Sea. They were well known in Bergen, and a long succession of Gotlanders are also mentioned in 13th century English customs records.

A whole variety of fraternities – religious and social organisations for merchants and, eventually, for craftsmen as well – were formed in Visby at this time. The German merchants brought with them their own organisational structure, known as the Hanse, which to begin with was a loose-knit federation to guarantee a monopoly of trade by means of privileges. This was the embryo of the later town Hanse, which in turn culminated in the mighty Hanseatic League, with Visby playing a leading role among the eastern member cities.

Stone upon stone

This escalation of trade meant growing prosperity for Visby's merchants, and the boom left its mark on the townscape once and for all. Streets and lanes were paved and quays were constructed. The pattern of settlement expanded steadily from the centre all through the Middle Ages. Growing trade and prosperity made it possible to build four-storey stone houses. This medieval type of house has only been found in one other Baltic town, namely Tallinn (Reval).

Typical street scene, looking down from Klinten. On the left, next to the Cathedral steps, is the house of Johan the Painter.

Such was the thickness of the new stone walls – up to a metre – that the small plots which had been occupied by the wooden settlement of the Viking era became too small. These were now amalgamated into larger plots, each equalling the width of a house. The massive crowstep gables of the façades faced the main street. At the top was a derrick, and the storeys below had openings for goods, as can still be seen in Strandgatan. The typical "packhouse" had a rectangular layout. The ground floor had one room, entered from the street. An external flight of steps and gallery led to the upper floors. The house had also privies with an internal channel down to a masonry latrine tank beneath the cellar. The packhouses, like the other settlement, extended inwards from the street in the form of continuous lines of buildings with living quarters at the rear. Only the living quarters had fireplaces.

For maximum space, houses were often joined together by arches over the narrow streets. Packhouses were also built outside the original town centre, but here there was more room and so the houses were often built with their sides, not their ends, overlooking the street. The whole area below Klinten is believed to have been built up by about 1300.

We know very little about the merchants' lives during this golden age in the city's history, and less still about housing conditions for the lower orders. The packhouses, starting point of the city's prosperity, are what have survived down to the present age, many of them much changed and rebuilt.

One of the town's courthouses, known as Vinkällaren (the Wine Cellar) or Kalvskinns-huset (Calfskin House), overlook the oldest square, Rolandstorget, where today Birger-gränd joins Strandgatan. The building itself has long since vanished, but its foundations survive under a more recent dwelling house. Calfskin House was an impressive masonry building, centrally located by the harbour. The council met here, and this was where all the town's wine was stored and dispensed.

The town wall

The most impressive monument from the days of Visby's greatness is the massive en-circling wall. Work on this began in about 1250 and was completed a hundred years later. Of all the medieval town walls in Europe, Visby's is one of the few still extant and one of the very oldest. It extends without a break for three-and-a-half kilometres from the old harbour round the inner city. Of the original 29 towers, 27 survive. Between them, the wall is set with smaller saddle turrets. There used to be 22 or 23 of these, but today only nine are extant.

Kruttornet (the Powder Tower), north of the old harbour, was probably built as a watchtower and fire-proof storage facility for the town and is probably Visby's first stone build-ing. The name dates from the 18th century, when the tower was the town's powder magazine. Sjömuren (the Sea Wall), extending from Donnersplats in the south by way of the sea-shore to Snäckgärdsporten in the north, was probably built quite soon after Kruttornet, to fend off attacks from the sea.

*Left: The encircling wall, more than three-and-a-half km long, is the best-preserved town wall in Northern Europe. It is divided into Nordermur (North Wall), Östermur (East Wall), Södermur (South Wall) and Sjömuren (Sea Wall). From this picture one can still sense part of the system of moats that once existed outside the wall.
Above: Popular walkway from the corner tower Silverhättan, along Nordermur.
Right: The gateway of Dalmanstornet, with its portcullis.*

The Sea Wall was originally six metres high, crenelated and with a wooden archers' platform.

This part of the wall had the biggest and most numerous gateways, but most of them have since been walled up. The wall on the landward side was built somewhat later, and to a different design. The archers' platform was a masonry structure surmounting a continuous arcade, still to be seen on the inside of the wall. In about 1300 the height of the wall was raised by three metres, and most of the towers date from this period. Seven gates gave

Left: Detail of the ruined church of St Hans.
Above: The ruined church of St Karin.
Right: Visby Cathedral, St Maria's Church, from the north-east.
Far right: This fantastic figure is a gargoyle on St Maria's Church.

the citizens access to the interior of the island. Outside the wall, up to three concentric moats were constructed, reinforced at certain points by dry stone walls.

Houses for the glory of God

Growing prosperity and booming trade were reflected, not only by secular buildings but by a spate of church building all through the 13th century. Even before 1350, Visby had no fewer than 17 churches and chapels. St Maria's Church, the present-day Cathedral, began building in the second half of the 12th century and is the only church that still has a roof on. With its huge western tower and its two small eastern ones, it dominates the surrounding settlement. The towers are a landmark, visible from far away. They give some idea of the impression Visby must have made, with the spires of now forgotten churches soaring skywards.

Population growth and rising prosperity also attracted various monastic orders

Previous spread: *Viewed from below, the arches of the ruined church of St Karin make a dizzying impression.*
Left: *Gravestone in St Karin's.*
Next page, top left: *View from Kyrkberget, with Dalmanstornet in the background.*
Top right: *Wisby Börs, one of the city's many medieval stone buildings with a typical crowstep gable overlooking the street.*
Bottom: *St Hansgatan, in the middle of old Visby, is a popular strolling area for the city's many summer visitors.*

to Visby. The ruins of the Dominicans' St Nicolaus and the Franciscans' St Karin show that these were churches of impressive proportions.

Town in transition

In about 1350, Visby's position in the Baltic trade was gradually weakened. Added to this, during the late medieval period Visby became a pawn in the turbulent politics of the Nordic countries. In 1361 Gotland was conquered by a Danish force commanded by King Valdemar Atterdag. Visby's trading privileges were confirmed by the Danish king, and the island remained Danish, with brief intermissions, for 300 years. For about ten years Visby was ruled by the Teutonic Order, which built the fortress of Visborg in the southern part of the city.

After parts of Visby had been torched by an army from Lübeck in 1525, neither the financial nor the human resources were available to rebuild its ruined houses and churches. The golden age of Visby was literally shattered. But Visborg, one of the greatest castles in Northern Europe, survived all the wars and tempests until the mid-17th century, and it was only in 1645, when Denmark surrendered Gotland to Sweden, that the last Danish castellan blew it up. Today only a few slight traces of it remain, near the town wall in the south.

In about 1650 the town began to grow again. The ruins were built on or cleared away, and new houses erected where the old ones used to be. In this way the medieval layout of the town was to a great extent retained. The northern part of Visby was redeveloped, and up on Klinten there emerged a settlement of humbler wooden buildings, mostly inhabited by craftsmen. German merchants and craftsmen settled in the town once again. For the first time since the 12th century, wooden houses were built in the old harbour area. Burmeisterska Huset, with its corner-jointed walls, is an outstandingly well-preserved specimen of Nordic wooden architecture in the 17th and 18th centuries. Both its decorations and the interior proclaim a very prosperous merchant family.

The new age

Visby's medieval settlement and ruined churches, unlike those of other Nordic towns, have been left undisturbed through the centuries. When the population grew, there were many house foundations inside the town wall to build on. In size these more recent houses differ little from medieval buildings, but their architecture and adornments are different. Many packhouses and medieval cellars are concealed behind façades of a later date.

Towards the end of the 19th century, new institutions became necessary, such as banks, schools and hospitals.

The growing tourist sector called for hotels and bathing facilities. New buildings were erected in the old city centre, but Visby's medieval architectural heritage became more and more widely known and appreciated, with the result that latter-day building activities inside the town wall were very limited.

With the onset of industrialisation at about the turn of the century, Visby was already highly appreciated for its architectural heritage. The town wall was placed under statutory protection already in 1808, and in the 1870s government grants were paid to keep the wall and the church ruins in good repair. A town plan, with a new configuration of streets, was drawn up in 1874 but rejected. Another plan, presented in 1912, was aimed at preserving the city intact within the encircling wall. A continuous green area was designated immediately outside the wall. New districts have all the time been developed outside this buffer zone.

In this way the inner city of Visby has been preserved as a unique historic setting. The continuing reflection of its age of greatness is due both to respectful treatment by the inhabitants and to the resilience of durable materials and solid craftsmanship. Thanks to the unusually well-preserved city centre, present-day strollers can gain a living picture of the Hanseatic town.

Top: One of the nine saddle turrets still extant. There used to be 22 or 23 of them.
Bottom: View towards Stora Torget and the ruined convent of St Karin.

The Rock Carvings in Tanum

Some people are making love to each other, while others seek solace with animals. Whole navies sail along the rock walls. Some of the ships have acrobats on board, while on others the crew stands stiffly to attention along the railing. Circles with rays cannot be anything but the solar disc. Someone is blowing a lur trumpet, other people seem to be taking part in a procession.

It has been a long time since Tanumshede could be reached by boat. Today the railway and the E6 European highway pass by this Bohuslän village. What is now flat land used to be an arm of the sea, with cobs and skerries. The first figures were scribed on smooth-worn rock faces about 3,200 years ago. In the course of a thousand years, many hundreds of rock faces in the surroundings of present-day Tanumshede were decorated with thousands of figures. And then it all ended, a few hundred years before the birth of Christ. The rock carvings were eventually entered in the biggest book of all – the book of oblivion. Similar carvings were executed in rocky slabs and outcrops all along the Kattegat and Skagerrak coasts to the Outer Oslo Fjord in the north. But nowhere else do they occur so close together and with such a variety of themes as round about the Tanum plain. Over 350 different sites have so far been discovered within the 45 km² of the World Heritage area. The four largest fields are open to visitors.

The people who once carved figures into the rock with hammer stones and stone chisels chose their sites carefully. The carvings occur on sloping rock faces on the sunny side, where the water lapped at the shoreline below and often trickled down the rock from above. Most of the rock faces are close to ancient arable or

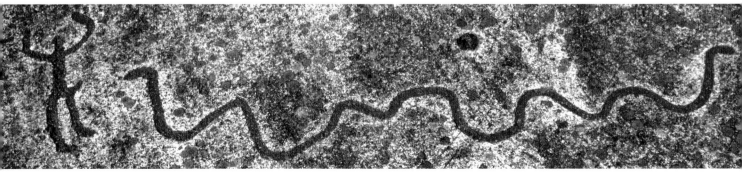

grazing land. All the carvings adjoin ancient settlements and burial grounds. None of them is located in inaccessible terrain or up on a ridge.

Tanum has carvings from a Bronze Age society with a settled population which tilled the soil and farmed cattle. The pictures describe what to us is a foreign world. Beings up to two-and-a-half metres tall rush forth from the rock brandishing spears. Most of them are men,

Page 45: Ships, warriors with swords, ancient symbols, shoe-prints – the rock faces of Fossumtorp abound in pictorial motifs.
Left, top: This loving couple, perhaps a bride and bride-groom, are depicted on the Vitlycke rock. The man wears a sword and the woman has tied her hair in a pony-tail.
Bottom left: The picture of the serpent and the man stretching his arms aloft, comes from the same rock face.
Above: These granite slabs outside Tanum are now next to a ploughed field. At the time of their carving, they were islands and skerries in a prehistoric archipelago landscape.

their members boldly and unashamedly erect. Women rarely occur, but are recognisable from the arrangement of their hair. Plaits and pony-tails were evidently fashionable. A magnificently antlered deer stands watching and listening, pushing against something we cannot see. Oxen occur, both singly and in groups. At one point they are pulling a plough, of the ancient kind called an ard. Horses were clearly not draught animals; they occur either singly or with a rider. Most of the carvings represent composite scenes. The Fossum rock presents a whole pictorial world, apparently created by one and the same person.

The rock carvings tell a story

The themes of the rock carvings are taken from the society in which they were created. Excavations of graves and settlement sites, among other things, tell us a certain amount about the life of these communities. The Bronze Age people of northern Europe have not left any

written documents behind them, and so we have to guess at the content and meaning of the rock carvings. For, quite clearly, it is not just everyday happenings that have been inscribed in the stone. Here we find no children and few women. We see warriors and their weapons, oxen, horses and whole processions, but never any everyday work. The many ships travelling along the rocks are often found in places which, even in Bronze Age times, were a long way away from the sea.

These works of art in the stone probably express people's beliefs and ritual acts. The many boats with their different crews can be variously interpreted. Do they represent a religious conviction, with the boat symbolising the vessel voyaging to the realm of the dead? Or are they symbols of power? Bronze and other luxury articles were

Above: The men in this carving at Bro Utmark are armed with lances, which they point at each other. The carving has not been filled in, and the rock surface is soft and smooth.
Right: On the south side of Aspeberget, a line of ships sail majestically through seasons and millennia.

much sought after by the social élite, and were mostly imported. So control over the means of communication – boats – was very important. Were the solar disc and the oxen symbols of fertility? The people sporting with each other are probably meant as participants in ritual acts. Depictions of the soles of feet, with or without shoes, can be interpreted as footprints of the gods, the gods themselves being too sacred for depiction. Or were they territorial markings?

The rock carvings can tell us about the ideas prevailing at this time, but nobody knows which powers people prayed to or what their gods were called. Perhaps the rock carvings were part of a wider context as cult locations. Some historians of religion have indicated a possible connection between the Nordic Bronze Age carvings and the later belief in the Aesir gods. Perhaps again there was a change of religion towards the end of the period, because several of the older carvings are covered over by new ones. The many armed figures on foot and horseback suggest that a military caste had emerged, as is also confirmed by burial finds.

Dating

The oldest of the Tanum rock carvings probably date from about 1800 BC, which makes them contemporaneous with the late Minoan period in Crete. The youngest of the Tanum carvings date from about 500 BC. The ma-

Left: This ship is on the rock face at Bro Utmark. After several thousand years, the marks left by the artist's carving stone are still clearly visible in the rock. Ships are a common theme of rock carvings, but nobody knows whether they have a religious background or are symbols of power. Do they represent ships sailing to the realm of the dead, or a bid to control the trade which was so important?

Below: Night-time photography at Litsleby, with trailing light – a technique which brings out the carvings in richly contrasted relief. All dealings with these rock carvings require great care, with a view to their future preservation.

jority belong to the period between 1000 and 500 BC, when Assyria held sway in the Middle East, the Olmec civilisation flourished in Central America and the Zhou dynasty came to power in China.

The height of the rock carvings above sea level provides some indication of their age. 3,500 years ago, the sea off Bohuslän came 25–29 metres higher up than it does today. The maximum age of the different rock carving sites can be deduced from what is termed isostatic

uplift – the elevation of the land following the retreat of the ice cap. They can at the very earliest have been created when the rock rose out of the sea. Implements, swords, bronze lur trumpets and oxen depicted can be compared with the corresponding, dated archaeological finds.

European context

Rock carvings are found in large parts of present-day Europe. But it is only in the Val Camonica in Italy that carvings have been found of the same extent and quality and from the same period as the Tanum ones.

The Fossum carving presents a plethora of human beings, animals and ships. The men are occupied fighting, while an armada sails over the rock. Footprints are common motifs. No one knows whether they are territorial markings or symbols of gods.

The many and varied motifs shed light on society, living conditions and beliefs during the European Bronze Age. Together with traces of settlements and burial grounds, the pictorial world of these rock faces testifies to a past era in a landscape which has been a human habitation for millennia.

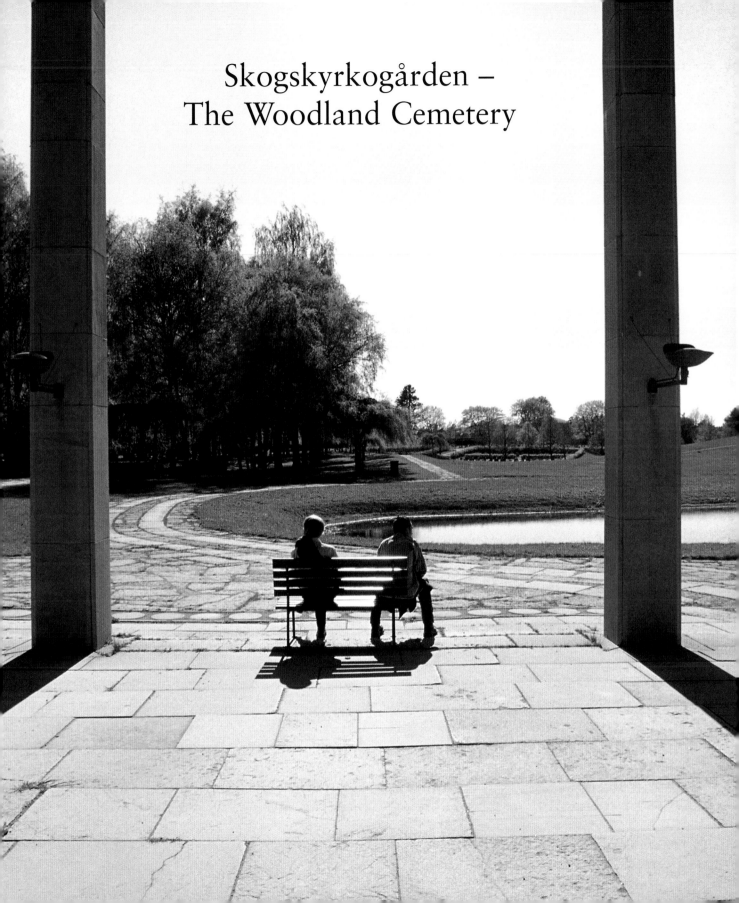

Skogskyrkogården –
The Woodland Cemetery

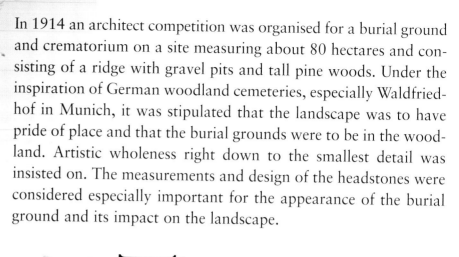

In 1914 an architect competition was organised for a burial ground and crematorium on a site measuring about 80 hectares and consisting of a ridge with gravel pits and tall pine woods. Under the inspiration of German woodland cemeteries, especially Waldfriedhof in Munich, it was stipulated that the landscape was to have pride of place and that the burial grounds were to be in the woodland. Artistic wholeness right down to the smallest detail was insisted on. The measurements and design of the headstones were considered especially important for the appearance of the burial ground and its impact on the landscape.

The tall granite cross is the first thing that catches your eye. The entrance to Skogskyrkogården is confidently shaped, with a walled road leading into an open landscape. A cinerarium lies behind white walls. A hill leads up to the chapels in the crematorium building, which is positioned like an elongation of the cinerarium. At the top of the rise, the granite cross soars heavenwards. The cross was an anonymous gift for the adornment of the place. It was designed by Gunnar Asplund, one of the two architects of Skogskyrkogården.

The other architect was Sigurd Lewerentz. Together they created a burial ground unique in architectural history and in cemetery art. Their beautiful and harmonious blend of natural scenery, parkland and architecture has been the exemplar of a succession of other burial grounds in many different parts of the world.

Genesis

Stockholm, like many other European capitals, experienced a tremendous growth of population at the end of the 19th century. Demand for burial places grew accordingly.

At the suggestion of one of the members of the cemeteries board, the architect competition was also opened up to foreign participants, making it the first international architects' competition in Sweden. By the closing date in April 1915, a total of 53 entries had been received. Most of them were traditional, park-like solutions. Gunnar Asplund and

Sigurd Lewerentz won the competition with an entry entitled "Tallum" – a Latinisation of *tall*, the Swedish word for pine. The scheme was for a building with a main chapel, inspiring reverence, and a crematorium to occupy the summit of the north-south ridge. This design was mainly an elaboration of Lewerentz' earlier sketch for a crematorium in Helsingborg. The burial ground, on the other hand, was designed in harmony with the original character of the place. The plans also included a number of smaller chapels and administrative and logistical buildings.

The winning entry was further developed in the years that followed. The existing gravel pits were to be terraced for burial grounds and a large open-air ceremonial point created for burials. Burial grounds and cinerarium were variously designed, adapted to the existing terrain and integrated with it. Drives and paths were laid out. The cinerarium adjoins one side of the main approach to the chapels, the Path of the Cross. Glades in the woods between and round the burial grounds admit sunshine and light between the pine tree shades.

The cremation movement

The basic idea permeating both the landscaping and the architecture was a ritual progress from darkness to light, from grief to reconciliation, from fear of death to courage for life. This idea was sustained by the cremation movement, which came to Sweden at the end of the 19th century as part of the social reform movements of the age. Urban population growth made cremation a matter of great hygienic significance, and the practice eventually came to be accepted both by the general public and by the Church. But the

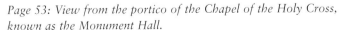

Page 53: View from the portico of the Chapel of the Holy Cross, known as the Monument Hall.

Left: The main entrance, the Path of the Cross, with the cinerarium on the left and the granite cross in the distance. The great cross, designed by Gunnar Asplund, was donated to the Woodland Cemetery by an anonymous benefactor.

Right: The cemetery landscape offers many small objects and elaborate details to dwell on.

cremation movement also demanded a funeral ceremony which was more humanist and less ecclesiastical in character. These tendencies coincided with the romantic naturalism of the turn of the century, thoughts which Lewerentz and Asplund fed into their work on Skogskyrkogården.

The Woodland Chapel

The first stage in the development of Skogskyrkogården was the Woodland Chapel (Skogskapellet), completed in 1920. Under the inspiration of country churchyards, Gunnar Asplund designed one with a small chapel looking eastwards in a tall pine wood as part of the main complex. Together with the underground mortuary right next door, this harks back

Above: The design and colouring of the Woodland Chapel is derived from the castle of Liselund in Denmark.
Below: Daylight aperture in the mortuary of the chapel.

to earlier, traditional building practices. The area is delimited by a low, distinct wall of rendered concrete. A narrow and deep-set entrance is surmounted by a relief inscription, *"Hodie mihi Cras tibi"* – Today me, tomorrow you. From this entrance a woodland path leads to the chapel door, which stands out in black and stern contrast against the white surfaces of the walls.

The steep, hipped roof of the chapel is tarred and shingled. The body of the building is low and rendered white, with the entrance retracted. Inside the outer door is a glazed double door with wrought-iron ornamentation.

Entering the white-painted ceremonial room of the chapel, one's eye is caught by a catafalque in the middle of the floor. Above this the roof is shaped like a dome, supported by eight pillars. Skylights in the dome admit daylight over the catafalque. The chairs, designed by Asplund, are positioned in two semicircles on either side of the catafalque and in one row along the side walls. The altar is positioned in a wide, low niche in the end wall, thus emphasising the catafalque and the deceased as the centre of attention. Whereas the entrance is characterised by the darkness of the conifer woods, the exit opens to the light.

The Resurrection Chapel

Skogskyrkogården was expanded in step with demand, but construction of the main chapel and crematorium kept being put off due to funding constraints. To ease

The interior of the Resurrection Chapel is pure and plain, its only decoration being the canopy and marble cross. The focal point of the room is the catafalque. The chairs were designed by Sigurd Lewerentz.

matters, a chapel, complete with chapel of rest and waiting room, was constructed in the southern part of the complex. This chapel, designed by Lewerentz, was consecrated in 1925 and named the Resurrection Chapel (Uppståndelsekapellet). Like the Woodland Chapel, it faces east, but it is entered from the north.

The Path of the Seven Pools, the axis linking the northern and southern parts of the cemetery together, ends at the Resurrection Chapel. The pools planned along the way were never constructed. The processional route through the tall pine wood leads to the chapel portico. The man-made, temple-like façade, with its pillars and heavy copper doors, makes a substantial contrast to the surrounding woodland.

The portico supported by beautiful columns with Corinthian capitals leads to the inside of the chapel, an airy, long, narrow room with a high ceiling. One row of chairs is positioned on each side of the catafalque, which is lit up by the one and only window. In the austerity of this room, attention is directed at the coffin on the catafalque which occupies the focus of attention.

The organ is placed high up over the exit at the west end, causing the sound to fill the room from above. Whereas tall, dark trees lead to a monumental entrance, the exit, on the contrary, is more modest, and faces a terraced burial ground surrounded by broadleaf trees.

Here as with the Woodland Chapel, the architecture and the landscape reproduce the ritual progress of the funeral from darkness to light.

The Groves of Meditation and Remembrance

From the Resurrection Chapel one glimpses a hill reminiscent of a prehistoric burial mound – the Grove of Meditation. As one follows the Path of the Seven Pools to this mound, the woodland changes character. Bright birch trees frame the height and the adjoining field. The Grove itself is surrounded by low walls.

Further east, beneath the hill, is an open-air ceremonial point, shaped like an amphitheatre in front of a limestone catafalque surrounded by six gas jets. A lily pond mirrors the sky, segregating the ceremonial point from the chapels and the Monument Hall at the end of the Path of the Cross.

The Grove of Remembrance, where ashes are interred in a common burial place, was opened in 1961.

The Chapels of the Holy Cross, Faith and Hope

Realisation of the crematorium and main chapel had been postponed time and time again for financial reasons. In 1935 a new master plan was drawn up for the

complex. One large and two smaller chapels were now to be built, with a crematorium, administrative and logistical facilities and a reception room. The assignment went to Gunnar Asplund. The building which emerged bore practically no resemblance to Asplund's and Lewerentz' original scheme. Twenty-one years had passed and architecture had acquired new ideals and a new vocabulary.

In front of the main chapel, the Holy Cross Chapel, is a large portico, the Monument Hall, with a flat roof supported by slender, square columns. John Lundqvist's sculptural group "The Resurrection" stands in the portico in front of the chapel, reaching towards the light through an opening in the roof.

Left: The Grove of Meditation with its fringe of massive elm trees. The tree tops along the horizon separate the open landscape from the conifer woodlands behind. In the Grove of Remembrance, to the right of the Grove of Meditation, the ashes of the dead repose in a common burial place.

Below: In the Monument Hall, John Lundkvist's sculptural group "The Resurrection" soars heavenwards, under an opening in the roof.

Previous spread: Its location on the summit of the ridge makes the Monument Hall visible from all the principal routes in the cemetery. And from here one can see all the different parts of "The Biblical Landscape", the ceremonial point, the lily pond, the Grove of Meditation and the Grove of Remembrance. Beyond the ridge is the City of Stockholm. Right: Grave quarters are gently imbedded in the scenery and the ground covered with gravestones instead of ling and blueberry shrubs.

The two smaller chapels, Faith and Hope, are north of the portico. The low walls and waiting rooms create intimate courtyards separating the chapels from each other and enabling mourners to wait in undisturbed privacy.

A glass wall with relief ornamentation separates the portico from chapel. This wall can be lowered clear if the Monument Hall is needed for especially large funerals.

Big windows facing south give the Chapel of the Holy Cross a shimmer of bright sunlight. The floor slopes down towards the catafalque, which almost completely obscures the low stone altar. The room expands towards the east and an arched end wall. This amphitheatre-like design is a reiteration of the ceremonial point outside. In this way the inner space links up with the outer one. Just as in the Woodland Chapel and the Resurrection Chapel, the catafalque is the centre of the room. The coffin stands against the mural "Life – Death – Life" at the far end, the theme of which is the leave-taking of the survivors on the shore, as the deceased puts out to sea.

When the Holy Cross Chapel was built, Asplund gained acceptance for his idea of a lift lowering the coffin into the crematorium. Because this chapel can also be used for "civil" funerals, the altar takes the form of a low stone plinth, decorated only with a small, plain cross which can be removed if so preferred. Whereas the painting in the east reflects the relationship between Life and Death, the glass wall at the west end of the chapel opens up on what Asplund called "The Biblical Landscape".

"The Biblical Landscape"

The view from the Monument Hall contains all the different natural elements of the complex: in the south, the graves in the grass, the fringe of bright birch trees, the tranquil darkness of the lily pond and the soft mounds by the ceremonial point. In

the north-west the ascending ridge, with its tall pine trees, screens off the city behind. Descending the slope towards the exit, one again passes by the cinerarium, which lies there like one of the cities of the dead in ancient Rome, re-created in Nordic form by Gunnar Asplund.

Each of the individual parts of Skogskyrkogården ranks as a milepost in the history of Nordic and European architecture, and the same is supremely true of the cemetery landscaping. Skogskyrkogården is a line of demarcation for burial places the world over. The entire complex, with all its various components, highlights what we are all subjected to, whatever our belief and religion: the individual person's life is but a tiny part of the great cycle of nature. Thus the great granite cross can be seen, not only as a Christian symbol but also as an emblem of Man's last resting place. As the poet Robert Hunter puts it: "Such a long, long time to be gone/and a short time to be here."

The Royal Domain of Drottningholm

In 1744, soon after becoming Crown Princess, Lovisa Ulrika received Drottningholm as a present from her father-in-law, Fredrik I. Work began almost immediately to refurbish the palace in accordance with the latest fashion. During the ensuing fifty years, Drottningholm expanded to its present-day proportions. Here Lovisa Ulrika accumulated her famous collections of insects and butterflies, her cabinet of coins and her library.

The beautiful pale-yellow palace is mirrored by the waters of Lake Mälaren. Behind it one glimpses the park, with its symmetrical, rectilinear formal garden. In the shade of the trees, paths wind across well-tended lawns. Small ornamented bridges traverse artificial ponds in the landscaped grounds. Close by the palace itself is the Drottningholm Palace Theatre, one of the few 18th century European theatres to have survived intact. On the outer fringe of the park is the Chinese Pavilion, remotely echoing the Orient.

Drottningholm makes a refined contrast to the rest of the Mälaren landscape of hills, rocky outcrops and conifer-clad horizon.

Drottningholm – "Queen's Island" – the place is aptly named, for a long succession of Swedish queens have held court here ever since the 16th century. Two of them are outstandingly associated with Drottningholm's evolution, namely Queen Hedvig Eleonora and, a few generations later, Queen Lovisa Ulrika.

The history of Drottningholm goes back to medieval times. It acquired its name at the end of the 16th century, when Katarina Jagellonica, King Johan III's Polish-born consort, resided here. It then changed hands several times. In 1661, one year after the death of Karl X Gustav, it was acquired by his widow, Hedvig Eleonora. Her tenure got off to an unfortunate start: the palace was burned to the ground that very same year. Work on the present building, designed by Nicodemus Tessin the Elder, began in 1662. Queen Dowager Hedvig Eleonora survived her late lamented husband by 45 years and devoted much of her time – and money – to Drottningholm. Huge sums were poured into building work, decorations, furniture and, not least, the grounds, but ample funds were forthcoming from her many estates in Central Sweden. Out of the ashes there rose a palace on contemporary European lines, emulating the Versailles of le Roi Soleil, Louis XIV of France.

Tessin died in 1681, but the work was carried on by his son and successor, Nicodemus Tessin the Younger, until the palace was finally completed in about 1700.

Previous page: This copy of the Apollo di Belvedere was acquired by Gustav III in Italy. The neoclassical façade of the theatre can be seen in the background.
Above: The east front of Drottningholm Palace.

The palace consists of a three-storey rectangular main building, flanked on the waterfront side by a couple of two-storey pavilions, also rectangular. The main building overlooks Lake Mälaren to the east and the park to the west. The wings, facing north and south, provide enclosed courtyards and are terminated by domed roundels. Their second storeys were added in about 1750.

In days gone by, visitors to Drottningholm always came by boat. The chosen ones would go ashore on the jetty downhill from the palace. The entrance is in the middle of the main building. The Tessins, father and son, with their confident mastery of dramatic effects, created

a portal and a stairway inspiring humility and respect. The entrance is sternly composed right down to the last detail. Tapering walls and the rising gradient of the floor make the corridor seem longer than it really is. The window overlooks the central axis of the park. The staircase is richly decorated with stucco work and mural paintings. Further west, the vestibules of the second and third storeys offer panoramic views of the park. Together with Hedvig Eleonora's State Bedchamber, the entrance and staircase are the most conspicuous features of Drottningholm's Baroque legacy.

Previous page: Karl XI's Gallery, with its beautiful painted ceiling. Eventually the ponderous Baroque gave way to a more light-hearted, French-inspired idiom.
Left: The Palace staircase is decorated with statues of Geatish kings and gods of classical antiquity.
Below: The upper vestibule faces west, offering a breathtaking view of the Baroque garden and grounds.

Above: This fountain, with a cast of a bronze statue by the Flemish master Adriaen de Vries, stands in the Baroque park.
Next page, above: Cartouche (scrollwork ornamentation) over a window of the Chinese Pavilion.
Below: Curved galleries on either side of the pavilion lead to the lower side pavilions, adding up to a horseshoe configuration.

The Baroque park

The park west of the palace conforms to the main outlines of the younger Tessin's garden design from the closing years of the 17th century. Here, as in the designs for the palace itself, Tessin was emulating the formal gardens of contemporary France, with Versailles as the paramount ideal. The main axis of the Drottningholm park is set at right angles to the mid-point of the palace façade, and to either side of it the park is divided into parterres – symmetrical fields, variously designed – ascending away from the palace.

Nearest the palace is the Embroidery Parterre (or knot garden). This has been greatly simplified with the passing years, until today it consists of lawns bordered by low, severely trimmed hedges and topiary shrubs. Both the terrace and the Embroidery Parterre are richly decorated with bronze statues of gods of classical antiquity. The statues we see today are casts of the originals looted by the Swedes in Prague in 1648 or captured in the war with Denmark in 1660. The originals themselves are housed in a museum a short way away from the palace. They are all by the same artist, Adriaen de Vries, and thanks to the fortunes of war, Drottningholm can boast the largest collection of works by this Flemish sculptor anywhere in Europe.

Behind the Embroidery Parterre is the Water Parterre, consisting of fountains backed by retaining walls and cascades. Beyond the cascades are the bosquets – low-level tree plantings in various configurations. The park continues with a large stellar bosquet, which has narrow paths radiating from its centre. What used to be small trees have now grown to be tall ones, obscuring the hill which makes a natural end point. Plans for expanding the Baroque park further north never materialised.

Turning south at the end of the Baroque park, one glimpses a pink building between the trees at the top of the ridge. On closer inspection this proves to be a small retreat with small pavilions to either side – the Chinese Pavilion. The main building consists of two storeys and curved galleries. In this way the Chinese Pavilion arcs

The Orient expressed

round the forecourt. Big French windows give it an open, airy atmosphere, while the roof and the copious reliefs enliven the façade, fully in keeping with the playful ideals of the Rococo. The exterior is consciously exotic, though the architecture, the decorations and the sur-

rounding parkland are unmistakably European. An 18th century Chinese would doubtless have recognised the read colouring and meander border of the façade, but he would quite certainly have been astonished by the positioning of the border on the outer wall. With a modicum of good will, perhaps he would have recognised the style. He would have nodded in recognition at the colour of the roof. This building must have been intended for the imperial family, since the façade ornaments are painted yellow, which is the colour of the sun and of the emperor. The octagonal entrance hall, with its marbled walls,

leads to the Mirrored Drawing Room and to the Red and Yellow Cabinet. The room designs are based on descriptions in contemporary travel books about China. Large porcelain urns and other Chinese works of decorative art contribute to the Chinese atmosphere. Much of the collection of porcelain figures in the library, upstairs, is also authentically Chinese.

The Chinese Pavilion was an expensive birthday present to Queen Lovisa Ulrika in 1753, from her consort, King Adolf Fredrik. The first Pavilion, though, quickly succumbed to rot and had to be pulled down. The present one, designed by Carl Fredrik Adelcrantz, was erected on the same site and completed in 1769. The decorations were done in Sweden, mainly after French originals.

The inspiration for the Chinese Pavilion came presumably from Prussia, where Frederick II (Frederick the Great), Lovisa Ulrika's brother, had a Chinese pavilion built at his castle of Rheinsberg in 1747.

For some decades the Chinese Pavilion was the royal family's summer residence, offering seclusion and informality. One of the side-pavilions had a dining room, the Confidence, where the table could be lifted up through the floor from the basement below, enabling the diners to converse undisturbed, *en confidence* – out of earshot of menials. The other side-pavilion housed the King's private lathe shop, where he spent hours fashioning what was perhaps a firmer yet more compliant material than the rest of his kingdom.

At the end of the 18th century the Pavilion lapsed into oblivion, but regular maintenance has preserved it for posterity.

The Chinese Pavilion was built as a French Rococo palace, after German precedent, designed by Swedish architects after patterns in an English book about Chinese architecture. The Orient has been completely reshaped in Europe's image, but the Red Cabinet inside the octagonal entrance hall has wall panelling of Chinese lacquer work and is tricked out with Chinese decorative art. Right: In the "Confidence" pavilion the royal family could talk without the servants hearing because the table, ready-laid, was hoisted up through the floor.

The theatre – a masterpiece

The Palace Theatre must be Drottningholm's most celebrated building. Lovisa Ulrika revelled in the cultural amenities and entertainments of her time, theatre and opera among them. The first Drottningholm theatre was built in 1754 but was destroyed by fire during a performance only a few years afterwards. Panic broke out because the evacuation of the building was hampered by the billowing gowns of the ladies.

The present theatre, completed in 1766, was designed by Carl Fredrik Adelcrantz, the architect of the Chinese Pavilion. It lies north of the palace, and is entered from the south side. It has a half-timbered frame and a rendered façade. It is very sparingly decorated, with just a moulding between the first and second storeys and a somewhat wider strip below the eaves. The entrance is discreetly accentuated by a frontispiece over the second storey, reminiscent of a Doric temple of classical antiquity.

The neo-classical idiom of the façade is reiterated by the interior, which is plain indeed, considering that it forms part of a royal palace. It is, nonetheless, an architectural masterpiece, with its poised, symmetrical balancing of stage and auditorium. The latter is the inverse of the deep stage, and the two are linked together by

Previous spread: The theatre foyer, which, during the last years of Gustav III's life, was extended towards the newly created "English Park", was originally Gustav III's Breakfast Room. The meals taken here were reserved for the innermost circle.

Left: The stage and auditorium are separated by the orchestra pit and the royal family's seats, visible at the bottom, in the middle of the picture. Complete stage sets for more than thirty different productions have survived intact since Gustav's time.

Right: Diana, Goddess of the Chase – one of the marble deities watching over "the English Park".

the orchestra pit and the royal seats at the front. Three boxes are symmetrically positioned on either side of the auditorium.

The heyday of the Drottningholm Palace Theatre came during the reign of Gustav III (1771-92), who actively encouraged the development of drama and opera in Swedish, billing it at Drottningholm as an alternative to the paramountcy of French. After his death the theatre went into suspended animation. It was barred up and used as a storage building. It was rediscovered in the 1920s, when, beneath inch-thick layers of dust, complete sets of scenery were found for over thirty different productions. The stage machinery was still intact – only the ropes needed replacing. The auditorium and stage were untouched. And so a complete 18th century theatre emerged, in full working order, from the shades.

"The English Park"

During the last years of Gustav III's reign the theatre foyer was extended towards the park on the south side. This part of the grounds had been landscaped after the contemporary English manner just a few years earlier, to create the impression of harmonious, virgin natural scenery. The principal component was a winding

Above: Flora, Goddess of Flowers, looks out over "the English Park".
Below: The façade of the theatre foyer puts one in mind of a Doric temple.

canal branching out into a system of lakes with islands and islets. Today the lakes are interspersed with undulating green lawns in the shade of huge trees. The paths meander – haphazardly as it seems – leading the visitor to one point of vantage after another. The tiny lakes provide glittering reflections of the surrounding parkland. An artificial burial mound – unfinished memorial to Gustav III – rises out of the water.

A unitary composition

The Gothic Tower – the only one of several intended park buildings to have actually materialised – stands on a mound in the park. From the top of it one has a view of the different parts of the Drottningholm complex. One sees the Baroque park, with its unity of diversity, and "the English Park", with its counterfeit "natural" scenery. All these elements make Drottningholm a rare and well-preserved example of a palace and grounds representing the stylistic ideals of the 17th and 18th centuries.

Birka and Hovgården

Most of the finds in the Black Earth are of an every-day nature, but they are no less important for that, because they tell us about the kinds of activity that went on in Birka. Archaeologists are seldom so elated as when they find old rubbish heaps, joyfully burrowing into things which people way back in prehistory just wanted to get rid of.

B irka, on the island of Björkö, was once among the first towns in Scandinavia. Today it is a country idyll. Travelling out to Björkö in Lake Mälaren, 30 km west of Stockholm, what you see in front of you is an open landscape, with meadows and plainlands spread out between birch-clad ridges and juniper-clad hills. Here there are thousands of small mounds, gathered in fields to either side of the open plain. The number of these burial mounds is unequalled in Northern Europe. In some places they are so close together as to resemble over-sized cobblestones. This is Birka's necropolis – the city of the dead. In Birka itself, on the northern half of Björkö, where people lived and worked, an open plainland slopes down to the water, with just a few earth ramparts on either side of a meadow betraying the presence, below ground, of what used to be a town.

Birka was founded in about 750 – we do not know exactly when or by whom. Two shipping lanes meet here: one linking Södertälje, on the coast further south, with Uppsala to the north, and the other connecting the interior of the Mälaren region with the eastern (Baltic) coast. Birka was carefully planned from the very outset, as can be seen from the pattern of settlement which the archaeologists have uncovered.

The monk Ansgar, Apostle of the North, came here for the first time in about 830 to preach Christianity, returning again in 852. The story of his life, written down in about 870, includes the

Previous page: The Black Earth – once a bustling trading town, now a rural idyll where nothing recalls the teaming activity existing here over a thousand years ago.
Right: In the area outside the Black Earth, Hemlanden, the small burial mounds are so close together that the ground seems to have goose pimples. Grave gifts and other finds in the mounds have taught scholars a great deal about the people of Birka, their religion and their social system.

living in Birka. A few years later, though, the priests were expelled, but the story of Ansgar's life and missionary activity gives us an insight into Birka's heyday. The town was a well-known, important trading centre in contemporary Europe. This is confirmed by finds unearthed during the past century on the site of the old town.

Treasures that glitter

Werner was a farm worker taking part in one of the first major excavations of the cultural layers of the town area. One autumn day in 1872 he unearthed an iron bowl full of silver coins, inscribed in unmistakable Arabic characters: "There is no god but Allah, and power is his alone." It is doubtful whether anyone in Birka at that time understood and appreciated this message, but silver was silver all the same. The silver coins came to Birka by way of the great rivers of Russia, along which merchants, adventurers and mercenary soldiers sailed to Imperial Constantinople and to the Realm of the Khazars on the Caspian Sea. Similar coins – more than 100,000 of them – found all over Scandinavia and in Russian territories testify to well-established trading routes and extensive trade and

oldest written information about Birka. We are told that it is in the Kingdom of the Svear, and is the town of their King. Ansgar was granted permission by King Björn to build a church in the town and appoint clergy, as well as baptising the town's "prefectus" or Governor. Ansgar was also welcomed by the Christian merchants and serfs

commodity exchange between Scandinavia, Eastern Europe and the Middle East.

The first scientific excavations had started the year before Werner made his discovery, but "digs" had already taken place at many of the burial mounds on Björkö during the 17th and early 19th centuries. Hjalmar Stolpe, the founder of modern Swedish archaeology, began excavating Birka in 1871. He headed an investigation of 1,100 burial mounds and of parts of what proved to be the old settlement – the Black Earth.

Grave goods recovered from different mounds, as well as differences in burial customs, have a great deal to tell us about their times. Cinerary graves are not a part of the Christian funeral tradition. Thor's hammer or a crucifix clearly tells us what people expected of the life hereafter, either Valhalla or Paradise. Jewellery, sewing things or weapons reveal the gender of the deceased, and the quantity of articles in the grave indicates his or her social standing. Jewellery and silk tell of trading relations with Central and East Asia.

Treasures that smell

Only a minor portion of the seven hectares of the Black Earth has been excavated. The cultural layers – the Black Earth created by human activity – are up to four metres in depth. They have been piled on top of each other like

settlement was a semicircular defensive rampart with a wooden palisade on top and with towers over the gates. It is the remains of this tenth century rampart that stand out between the plain and the burial ground in Hemlanden ("the Home Lands"), to the east of the town.

In addition to the fortifications surrounding the settlement, a stronghold was built which is still partly visible up on the height. This fort, which was presumably garrisoned, had the same kind of defences as the town beneath: ramparts four metres high with a wooden palisade on top.

Trade and crafts

At most, Birka had over a thousand inhabitants. Life here must have been completely different from the surrounding countryside. To live by agriculture you needed cultivable land and access to grazing, either on your own behalf or someone else's. In Birka things were different. People lived here in an advanced, specialised economy segregated from the agrarian society.

Birka's economy was based on trade and crafts. At the beginning of its history, most of the trade routes went to the southern Baltic and Western Europe. Birka mainly exported furs, but also iron and various craft products. Trade routes changed in the 9th century. Arabic silver coins, textiles, glass beads and jewellery turn up in the finds from this period. Not all luxury articles came to Birka as a result of trade. Some were loot and taxes brought home from the east.

The many finds of tools and craft products tell us that Birka was not just a trade centre. There were highly specialised craftsmen living here as well. Innumerable moulds for jewellery have come to light. Elegantly crafted bone combs and other articles of bone and horn show that comb-makers were also active here. Birka-type combs have also been found in other Viking towns, from York and Dublin in the west to Staraya Ladoga, near what is now St Petersburg, in the east.

Birka probably had other craftsmen too, such as boat builders, sail-makers and stevedores. The citizens had to eat, so Birka must have had butchers and bakers as well.

the growth rings of a tree and, consequently, make excellent points of reference for dating. Even a modest potsherd will for the most part reveal when and where it was made, and its position in the cultural layer tells us when it was discarded. Potsherds and suchlike tell us about the types of goods people traded in at different times. Bone fragments and kitchen waste tell us what was on the menu.

Only the house foundations remain, but they tell us that the houses were built using a technique resembling the half-timbering of later ages. The plots in the town were demarcated by ditches and alleys. On terraces near the town rampart, several long houses of a familiar Nordic type made up a kind of "suburb".

The fortified town

When the town began to be built, the sea came about six metres higher up than it does in the present-day Mälaren region. Birka's harbour occupied a crescent-shaped bay. The settlement near the harbour was fan-shaped, with the ends of the houses facing the harbour, just as they do in the later medieval towns of Visby and Bergen. Streets and lanes, paved with wooden planks, radiated from the harbour and in between the houses. Some of them extended, as piers, into the pool itself.

Birka was eventually fortified, on both the seaward and landward sides. Traces of piles in the water show that the inlet was blocked by them, with just small openings in between for boats to enter and leave by. Behind the

Left: The Birka Museum, opened by King Carl XVI Gustaf in 1996, displays in a permanent exhibition a model of Birka and the King's banqueting hall at Hovgården on the island of Adelsö. Many of the finds from the excavations are also to be seen here.

This page: Model-maker Lars Agger has re-created Birka with all its activities, different types of settlement, trades and occupations. Seen through the eyes of both children and adults, the old town comes to life again.

Next spread: Birka is a popular destination in spring and summer. Pictured here is a school party walking along the crest of the Borgvallen rampart.

Left: The rune-stone on Adelsö stands down by the old harbour. It is decorated in "Urnes" style, and the winding text is the oldest known writing in Sweden with the words "King" and "Roden", i.e. Roslagen.
Above: The remains of Alsnö Hus, opposite Birka on the island of Adelsö. This royal manor was built in the 13th century and was one of the first secular brick buildings in Sweden.

Relations with the monarchy

The King of the Svear had a Governor stationed in Birka to keep an eye on things and also to guarantee the merchants' security. Most of the indications are that Birka was planned and created on the initiative of a monarchy, which in Birka's case meant the King of the Svear.

Standing by the shore where Birka's harbour used to be, you look across to Adelsö, the neighbouring island to the north. Opposite Birka are the remains and foundations of a royal manor of the same age as the early Birka township. The location of the royal manor can hardly be a coincidence. The view across the strait is magnificent, today as ever. A line of big burial mounds close to the royal manor is also visible from Birka. The mounds are somewhat later than the manor. There is much to suggest that the royal manor and Birka were founded as parts of a single plan for securing long-distance trade to the area.

Towards the end of the 10th century, after 200 years of prosperity, Birka fell into decay. Its decline forms part of a pattern: other European towns also disappeared at this time. There were several reasons, most of them economic and social. In Birka's case the decline can also be connected with the introduction of new and larger ships. The old sailing route from the south, by way of Södertälje, was no longer navigable. The big ships had to sail into Lake Mälaren from the east. The King of the Svear moved both his headquarters and urban activity to Sigtuna. The German historian Adam of Bremen tells us that by about 1060 Birka was "so desolate that hardly a trace of the town is visible".

Excavations of this deserted landscape are still going on. Finds in recent years have included a horseman buried beneath the fort rampart together with a stallion. The same investigation established that the fort had been destroyed by fire at least three times. The garrison, a 180 m² house for Birka's crack troops, has also been excavated.

Hovgården – the royal manor on Adelsö

The royal manor on Adelsö, *Hovgården*, survived Birka's disappearance. In the 11th century, an ornate stone with a runic inscription was erected by the old harbour. It stands there to this day, adjuring us: "Tell the runes. Rightly did Tolir, Steward of Roden, scribe them for the King. Tolir

and Gylla had (these runes) inscribed, both spouses, to their memory ... Håkon bade scribe." This inscription is a centrepiece of Swedish medieval studies. The stone provides further evidence of royal domination here. The present stone church was built towards the end of the 12th century, probably for the manor.

A hundred years later, a massive building was erected over the ruins of the old royal manor as one of the first secular brick buildings in Sweden. At the same time the old harbour was enlarged. *Alsnö Hus* (Alsnö Palace), at the summit of Adelsö, was the scene of a long succession of diets or parliaments. It was here that the leaders of the realm gathered in about 1280 and, under the direction of King Magnus Ladulås, adopted the Alsnö Statute, granting the nobility tax exemption in return for military service. This established the nobility as a separate estate. Ruins are all that remains today of Alsnö Hus, but a vestige of the landed nobility's tax exemption survived to the beginning of the 20th century.

Hemlanden is the necropolis of Birka, where the burial mounds lie close together in the birch wood. Funeral rituals and grave gifts tell the stories of the dead. Jewels were given to women, weapons to men and toys to children. A cinerary grave, in which the body was buried after cremation, suggests that the deceased was not Christian. The cross and the hammer of Thor reveal expectations of a life to come. Costly gifts are found in the graves of the affluent, humbler gifts suggest lower status in life.

The Engelsberg Ironworks

On 11th April 1738, Erik Månsson, a forge hand, was hauled before the court by ironworks proprietor Söderhielm, charged with stealing about 15 kilos of bar iron. He was ordered to pay 4 *daler* and 12 *öre* damages and sentenced to a flogging.

The Engelsberg ironworks – Engelsbergs Bruk – belong to Sweden's "Age of Greatness" as a major European power in the 17th and 18th centuries. The noise of the blast furnace, the rushing of the waterfall and the clanking of the hammer forge were heard at Engelsbergs Bruk, and the air was rank with perspiration, charcoal and smoke. At Engelsberg, and hundreds of manufactories like it, iron ore was smelted and forged into steel. This was a vital part of the economy and the military technology underpinning Sweden's Baltic Empire. Swedish steel and iron dominated Europe until about 1750, when coal began to be used in the English iron and steel industry.

Ängelsberg is in the municipality of Fagersta, in the province of Västmanland, just a few hours' journey north-west of Stockholm. Engelsbergs Bruk is on the river which flows from Lake Snyten to the larger Åmänningen. Low, red-painted timber buildings are scattered about, peacefully surrounded by large broadleaf trees. The blast furnace and roasting furnace, compactly built, make a more dominant impression. As a contrast, there is a small summerhouse by the pond close by, and the idyll is reinforced by the park on either side of the avenue leading up to the manor house. Two circular, domed slagstone pavilions flank the *corps de logis*. The courtyard is bounded by two red-painted timber wings with hipped roofs, set at right angles to the manor house itself, enthroned at the far end of the manufactory. The manor house is painted white and has two storeys, with a clock tower on the Mansard roof and columns marking its entrance.

Page 91: Roofs of the melting furnace and blast furnace.
Left: The two round, domed slagstone pavilions below the entrance to the manor house are called the Pleasure Dome (Lustgården) and the "All Alone" (Nödgården), the first being a summerhouse, the second a privy. The beautiful blue slagstone is a partly vitrified waste product from the manufactory's blast furnace. Slagstone is a common building material in Bergslagen.

The ochard behind it used to be a symmetrical park with an orangery.

Herrsmedjan – the manorial forge – which used to be the estate's "gold mine", stands close to the manor house. Both its position and its rendered and decorated slagstone façade tell us that it was the bar iron from the forge, not the crude iron from the furnace, which paid best. The workers' homes were a good deal more modest and were located on the periphery of the estate, at a respectful distance from the manor house.

Background

Iron was already being extracted in Norberg before the Christian era. Right down to the present day, abundant deposits of iron ore in Central Sweden have laid the foundations of widespread metalliferous mining. Lake and bog ore was melted in blast pits, the oldest of which in this area dates back 2,300 years. Open-cast mines were constructed in the rock in about 1100, using a technique known as fire-setting, whereby the rock was heated with big fires and then hastily cooled with water, so that it cracked and could then be broken up. The introduction of water power at the end of the 13th century made possible the extraction of ore on a bigger scale. Operations of this kind had two prerequisites: forests, supplying wood for the big fires and charcoal for the furnaces, and water power to drive the bellows.

Innumerable blast furnaces were constructed alongside watercourses. The yeoman-miners – *bergsmän* – joined forces in *bergslag*, which originally meant a working team and a mining area. The Norberg *bergslag*, of which Engelsbergs Bruk forms part, is the oldest

Above: A factory street in Engelsberg. The building on the right used to be a piggery, cow shed and lime shed.
Right: One of the three waterwheels of Herrsmedjan (the manorial forge). Built in about 1840, this forge is the sole survivor of the three which the manufactory once numbered.

known in Sweden. Engelsberg is first mentioned in written records in about 1300, but as Englikebenning – Englike's building or dwelling. Englike was a German immigrant, grandfather of the rebel and subsequently Captain-General Engelbrekt Engelbrektsson.

Englikebenning becomes Engelsberg

A large furnace was eventually constructed, and in 1597 the first Herrsmedjan was in place, next to the two blast furnaces here. In 1681 parts of the area were acquired by Per Larsson Höök. He went on to purchase additional properties in the locality – forest, hammer forges and furnaces. This marked the beginning of more than

200 years' operations under the name of Engelsbergs Bruk. Höök, who was later raised to the nobility and took the name of Gyllenhöök, never lived here himself and no sizeable manor house was built here in his day. The east wing of the present manor house is the oldest building. It was constructed, as the manager's living quarters, in about 1700. The main building came fifty years later. That too is corner-jointed, but with boarding both inside and out. The west wing was built in the 1780s to resemble the east wing. It is traditionally said to have been built to accommodate the many children of the then proprietor, Lorents Petter Söderhielm.

The apogee

Between 1695 and 1767 the estate raised its annual output from 135 to 264 tons. The forge and furnace we see today were built in 1778-79. This is a timber-clad furnace. Its refractory stone stack is insulated with earth

and gravel and faced with timber and stone secured with iron hoops. The furnace was enlarged in 1836, when a water-powered blower was fitted, improving both the fuel economy and the output. The roasting furnace was added twelve years later. In it the ore was heated and purified before being crushed and sent for melting. The roasting furnace was heated with the exhaust fumes from the blast furnace.

The water wheel drove an ingenious system of shafts, wheels and chains for pulling sleds of ore to the top of the roasting furnace and charcoal to the top of the blast furnace. Herrsmedjan was built of slagstone gravel in about 1840, and most of it is occupied by the rough forge. The hardening furnaces, representing the first stage in the conversion of the pig iron to malleable iron were twice renewed, most recently in the 1880s, when the two Lancashire hearths were fitted. Two bar iron hammers, powered by a waterwheel, forged the iron into bars of

Left page, top picture: The pond behind Herrsmedjan harboured the manufactory's lifeblood – water.
Left page, bottom picture: The pig iron was tempered in the furnace, as the first stage in upgrading it to malleable iron.
Above: The melting furnace with Council cottage, blast furnace, roasting furnace and charcoal conveyor.
Below: The east wing is the oldest building, dating from about 1700 and originally the manager's living quarters.

a predetermined weight and size – *bergslag* weight. The bar iron – the estate's end product – was extremely valuable. At times it was legal tender. To an impoverished worker, it must have been very tempting to help oneself to a piece of bar iron. Thefts of iron are the dominant offence in the records of the mine court.

Sunset and swansong

Despite repeated modernisation in the mid-19th century, Engelsbergs Bruk was left standing by the onward march of technology. Charcoal-based iron production was knocked out by coal firing and more advanced upgrading processes. The Engelsberg forge was shut down in 1890. The owner, Clas Gabriel Timm, leased the buildings to Fagersta Bruk, which kept the ironworks going until 1916. Timm then sold the estate to Avesta Jernverk, which belonged to Consul-General Axel Ax:son Johnson. Heavy demand for timber and iron during the First World War gave the estate a period of grace. A new forge was built in 1917 and today houses an engineering workshop.

By 1919, the sands of time had definitely run out for the manufactory. It had lived to a ripe old age, but now it was quite out of date. Axel Ax:son Johnson, an eminent shipowner and industrialist, mothballed the estate when the blast furnace was shut down, and so it has remained, nearly untouched, with about fifty different buildings. Time was when blast furnaces and other buildings for iron working were a common sight in Bergslagen. Today very few indeed survive. No manufactory is anything like as complete and well-preserved as Engelsbergs Bruk. The charcoal shed, which used to stand next to the furnace is all that has been demolished. That was in the 1960s, at the same time as the

This rusty old gear wheel lies on the bank of the pond behind Herrsmedjan (the manorial forge). The pond and the forge are straight downhill from the manor house, indicating that the activities of the forge were what mattered most.

big cowshed was turned into archives for the records of the Johnson conglomerate. Those records include the historically very valuable and extensive archives of Engelsbergs Bruk, relating to 600 years of activity.

The estate buildings, complete with forge and furnaces, stand today as unique, well-preserved monuments to an industrial process.

The Mining Area of the Great Copper Mountain in Falun

"Anyone wishing to visualise the whole of this mine must imagine a murky chasm, terrible and deep ... sustained by itself alone, full of lighted fires, full of smoke, of sulphur and of metallic odours, full of dripping water. And then, in the bowels of the earth, blackened human beings, looking like imps of Hell, the echoes of hammers and crowbars, the shouts of the miners ... and last of all the destruction and the infernal noise that can result from such a fearful, ponderous work collapsing."

Charles Ogier wrote this eye-witness description of the Stora Kopparberget ("Great Copper Mountain") mine in Dalarna during the mid-1630s, while serving as French envoy to Sweden. The mine and its surroundings are a unique, wholly man-made landscape. The World Heritage site includes not only the thousand-year-old mine itself but also several furnace sites, as well as watercourses, hammer ponds, large areas of farmland, and several homesteads associated with the *bergsman* (yeoman-miner) class. Then there is the town of Falun, which received its charter in 1641. This is one of the biggest wooden towns in Sweden, with many buildings dating as far back as the 15th century. Falun in its day was the second largest town in Sweden, with a population of six thousand.

Below ground, the Stora Kopparberget mine has galleries and shafts anything up to 400 metres below the surface. Above ground it includes hoisting gear, head frames, wheelhouses, winch houses, offices, living quarters and a variety of other buildings dating from the 17th, 18th and 19th centuries. The area surrounding the mine is dominated by mountainous piles of waste rock.

Earliest times

No one quite knows when copper ore first began to be extracted here, but present-day archaeologists and geologists believe that it was already being mined in the 8th

century. The ore was discovered by farmers. One myth has it that a goat called Kåre returned home one day with his horns tinged red, which aroused his owner's curiosity. The farmer went into the forest and found the place where Kåre had been grubbing, and the ore deposit with it.

The first written mention of the copper mine comes in a letter in 1288, confirming that the Bishop of Västerås has acquired an eighth part of the "Mountain" in return for extensive, prosperous lands. Clearly, then, the mining operation at Tiskasjöberg was no longer the exclusive, small-scale concern of the local farmers. An orga-

Page 99: The Great Pit resulted from a collapse in 1687, when large parts of the mine caved in.
Left: The yellow building on the brink of the Great Pit is the Great Mine Cottage, dating from the 1770s.
Right: "The Horse Steps". The workhorses were stabled in the mine and hardly ever saw daylight.

nisation now existed whereby shares in the enterprise could be bought and sold, and the social élite were heavily involved. From medieval times and for many centuries thereafter, Stora Kopparberget was Sweden's most remunerative business undertaking. As a result, the *bergsmän* grew wealthy, powerful and self-conscious.

The technology

For a long time – it might have been several centuries – the farmers engaged in what can best be termed domestic mining. The ore was extracted in open pits – haphazardly, wherever the vein seemed richest.

From at least the beginning of the 13th century and until the end of the 18th, ore was extracted and dressed using essentially the same technology. The first stage was fire-setting. Big fires were lit against the rock, making it brittle and easy to break. During the early centuries the ore was conveyed to the surface with primitive winches and capstans. Starting in the 16th century, technology and installations were modernised along German lines, until in the 18th century there came another great leap forward, putting Sweden in the international forefront

Well into the 18th century, ore was still being extracted by the same primitive technique and with the same tools as in medieval times. With pick axes, crowbars and shovels, the mine labourers laid the foundations of Sweden's prosperity in the 17th century "Age of Greatness".

of mining technology. Blasting was introduced, and productivity skyrocketed.

Once the ore had been conveyed to the surface, the ensuing processes were both time-consuming and complicated. First the ore had to be roasted, to remove most of its sulphur content. This was done out in the open, with the ore left burning for weeks on end. The thick plumes of smoke from the roasting fires soon became one of the main distinguishing characteristics of the Falun district, along with the sterile landscape all around. Buildings were blackened by soot and eventually nothing, not even moss, would grow in this ever-grimier slag-ridden wilderness.

The roasted ore, now broken up and desulphurised, was melted in a furnace. During the mine's heyday, in the 17th century, there were about 140 furnaces. They were water-powered, and for their sake an entire aquatic landscape of ponds, canals and ditches had come into being.

For several centuries Sweden was the world's biggest producer of copper, with Stora Kopparberget accounting in the mid-17th century for two-thirds of the whole world's output. No wonder, then, that, as the government of the day put it, "The Kingdom stands or falls by Kopparberget."

The bergsmansgård at Gamla Staberg has a history going back to medieval times, and its garden, now in the process of restoration, still shows traces of Baroque ideals. One of the wings has been turned into a museum.

In the country round about the mine, the wealthy, powerful yeomen-miners (bergsmän) had magnificent manorial residences built for themselves, many of which are now included on the World Heritage List. One of them is Sveden, home of Linnaeus' in-laws, where he and his wife, Sara Lisa, were married in 1739. Several other famous men have lived there since, among them Emanuel Swedenborg.

The mining aristocracy created magnificent homes expressing "the peculiar blend of stern simplicity and exuberant, indiscriminate social-climbing which was their hallmark".

Organisation

Out of a random, haphazard operation there evolved an ownership structure which survived more or less intact until the end of the 19th century, the Stora Kopparberget *bergslag*. This was a corporate activity in which the *bergsmän* owned shares, termed "fourth parts". The *bergsmän* were the region's aristocracy. Together with a royal bailiff, they made all the decisions on mining operations.

The early 16th century was a trying time for the *bergsmän* of Falun. The mine was yielding less and less and activities were being more and more closely controlled from Stockholm, but worst of all, a long succession of collapses claimed lives and made parts of the mine almost inaccessible and waterlogged. But the closing years

Previous spread: The Adolf Fredrik pithead building was constructed in 1845 over the 280-metre-deep Adolf Fredrik shaft. Since then it has been moved to another position in the mine area.
Left: Stora Kopparberg's beautiful slagstone building in Mariegatan, Falun, contains many items of historic interest.
Right: A school party, protectively clothed, visiting the Hall of Universal Peace.

export profits to grow exponentially. Mining operations, like the organisation itself, were modern by the standards of the time, Sweden dominated the world's copper trade and business had never been better.

The ore itself was extracted in huge galleries, tier upon tier of them. Galleries and adits were separated by floors, pillars and walls which were all the time being weakened by fire-setting and by the policy of extracting as much "pay dirt" as possible. Walls and roofs grew steadily thinner and collapses were constantly occurring, some of the very worst of them in 1635 and 1655. But the miners soldiered hectically on in the richly remunerative galleries, the load-bearing walls were made thinner and thinner and catastrophe closed in. At about Midsummer 1687 the mine began ominously creaking, and on 25th June the earth trembled and the air was filled with a deafening roar as the partition wall between the two main pits crumbled into one huge chasm, obliterating the floors and galleries beneath. After the dust had settled, people could look out over what today is known as Stora Stöten, the Great Pit. The chasm was over a hundred metres deep, but the rubble at the bottom of it was another 80 metres thick. By a miracle, no lives were lost, all the workers having downed tools for the Midsummer celebrations.

Decline

Exports of copper declined seriously in the 18th century, but, thanks to the introduction of blasting technology, production could be sustained at the mine and Sweden still led the world in mining technology and mechanics. The drudgery of a thousand pit workers at this time is

of that century saw big initiatives and modernisation measures which laid the foundations of the mine's real heyday in the 17th century. In 1650 there were over 600 *bergsmän* with shares in the enterprise, nearly a thousand people were employed in the mine itself and output of crude copper, over 3,000 tons, broke all records. In 1619 a copper refinery was established at Säter, causing

THE MINING AREA OF THE GREAT COPPER MOUNTAIN IN FALUN

depicted in several well-known paintings by Pehr Hille-ström (1732-1816).

More disasters were to follow as the 18th century wore on. Falun was ravaged in 1761 by two big fires which also took their toll of the mining installations.

In the 1780s Gustav III gave permission for a silver refinery to be established at the mine, and the Falun silver mine returned handsome profits until as recently as the 1920s. A silver furnace dating from 1884 and still intact can be visited today. Mining operations changed and were now made to focus on other substances, and the mine's prosperity now came to depend on sulphur, zinc and lead, as well as silver and gold. Falun now also acquired a chemical industry, with vitriol, sulphuric acid, distilled vinegar *(ättika)* and Falun red paint as its best-known products, though the biggest and most important product of all was iron pyrites.

By the end of the 19th century all the copper furnaces were abandoned and new industries had succeeded them. The Stora Kopparberget mine was still operational when its heptacentenary came round in 1988, but on 8th December 1992 the last charge was fired and the mine closed down for good. A mining museum, though, had already been created in 1922, and in 1970 part of the old mine was opened up to visitors.

The mine and the installations surrounding the Great Pit are among the oldest and most important mine workings in the world. For centuries, the "Great Copper Mountain" spurred and influenced both the international economy and mining technology.

Long, straight streets are typical of Falun's old layout. This one, Åsgatan, is lined by 18th century wooden houses.
Next page: Entrance to the tourist mine. The symbols over the entrance represent the ores and minerals of the mountain. In the middle, gold. The two on the right are silver and lead, the two on the left are iron and copper. In addition, iron and copper vitriol, sulphur, zinc and steel. The circle with three dots represents the classic "Swedish Red" paint made in Falun.

The Mining Area of the Great Copper Mountain in Falun

Höga Kusten – The High Coast

Forty days and forty nights it rained, until the whole earth was inundated. God then commanded the water to recede, and it did so in no uncertain manner. Learned men still knew for a certainty at the beginning of the 19th century that it was due to the subsidence of the waters that the shoreline appeared to be moving progressively further out with the passing of time. It was not until the end of the 19th century that scientists discovered the geological phenomenon of isostatic uplift, though its effects had been known to man for centuries, with a good number of coastal communities and fishing villages, especially in Norrland, eventually finding themselves "high and dry".

During the last Ice Age, the land was depressed by the weight of the ice, rising again when the ice melted and the weight was removed. Isostatic uplift means the land rising "of itself". It's rather like poking a hole in bread dough. Pull out your thumb, the dough rises and before long the surface will be smooth and even again. Uplift can also be tectonic, in which case the ground is pressed upwards by the pressure from two plates of the earth's crust being pressed together.

Three kilometres of ice

The Scandinavian ice cap reached all the way down to the region of Berlin in the south, Moscow in the east and westwards out into the Atlantic. Twenty thousand years ago it was up to 3,000 metres thick. Millennium after millennium this colossal burden of ice bore down upon the land surface. At most the thickest and heaviest part of the ice cap depressed the land more than 800 metres below the present sea level. This "ice dome" centred on the province of Ångermanland and Höga Kusten (the High Coast). Ten thousand years ago the climate turned warmer

Page 111: On the western side of Skuleberget, the rock has been washed clean by the waves. The ground on which the house stands once lay far below the water level.
Right: From the summit of Slåttdalsberget the effects of isostatic uplift are clearly visible. The two lakes were once the inside of an arm of the sea. As the land rose, the bay became silted up and, eventually, was cut off from the sea.

and the ice melted and retreated. Relieved of its pressure, the land rose. This uplift was fastest immediately after the ice melted, then it gradually slowed down. The edge of the ice reached Höga Kusten 9,600 years ago, and the land there is still rising at a rate of 8 mm annually.

The natural scene has been transformed many times with the passing millennia, and flora, fauna and human beings have adapted to the changes. Immediately after the ice melted, this region lay under the sea. Scattered islands rose above the water to begin with, forming an archipelago landscape in a sea full of icebergs. Those islands were the peaks of mountains more than 285 metres high. They are visible in the present-day landscape as "till-capped hills" – their tops tree-clad, and their sides washed clean by the waves. The bare cliff face of Skuleberget has the world's highest shoreline, 285 metres above sea level. These hills are only 2 or 3 kilometres from the present shoreline as the crow flies. The entire Höga Kusten region is very hilly and traversed by fault scarps, long valleys and deeply incised bays. The water in the archipelago is over a hundred metres deep. This dramatic topography serves to articulate and concentrate the effects of isostatic uplift.

Nature in transition

The "caps" of the highest mountain peaks consist of till, a soil which includes everything from fine clay to large, angular boulders. The till was left behind when

When the land rose out of the sea, the finer material was rinsed away but larger and heavier stones were left lying on the beach. Along Norrfällsviken, the shingle fields of the future are now taking shape, the biggest being 550 metres long and 250 metres across. Higher up in the terrain are several Bronze Age cairns constructed of shingle on what was then the shoreline.

the retreating ice cap moved over the land like a huge piece of sandpaper. The soil beneath the water was eroded by the force of the waves – "wave-washed". The debris washed out of the till by the waves was deposited on the seabed: heavier material settled near the coast, lighter particles were carried further out to sea by the currents. Because isostatic uplift has been going on without interruption for a long time, the same soil masses have been processed and shifted several times over.

The biggest stones are called shingle, and were deposited in ridges at different heights along the mountain sides. These wave-washed shingle fields are a magnificent sight, with many different rocks and lichens presenting a motley array of colours and the stones themselves worn smooth and even by the water. The Högklinten mountain has the world's highest shingle field, 260 metres above sea level.

Beneath a shingle field there are massive accumulations of gravel and sand. These too were formed by the water washing over the soil. Between four and six thousand years ago the then waterline was inhabited by huge numbers of molluscs and mussels. Their shells became embedded in the sand deposits, and in present-day sandpits these are visible as beautiful, brilliant white and mauve stripes in the sand. Deeper down in the valleys, which, thousands of years ago, were arms of the sea, the finest sand and clay accumulated, and it was here that men eventually found good cultivable soil.

With the passing millennia, the sea and the long-narrow bays became progressively shallower. At narrow, shallow passages and inlets the bays were cut off from the sea, becoming freshwater lakes. Because isostatic uplift is still going on, some of these lakes will eventually become more and more shallow and be choked with vegetation, forming wetlands. Slåttdalsmyren is a clear illustration of the shape of things to come. Nine thousand years ago it was an arm of the sea, but eventually it was cut off and became a small lake. As isostatic uplift

continued, the lake became progressively shallower until in the end it dried out. Today it is a small wetland 200 metres inland.

As a result of human beings trailing the retreating shoreline, Bronze Age cairns, Iron Age settlement sites and medieval fishing camps, for example, are to be seen at various altitudes in the landscape. This way it is easy to study how people lived, because more recent cultural layers have not been superimposed on older ones, as is usually the case.

Man follows the coast

The first hunter-gatherers had already come to Höga Kusten eight thousand years ago. For many thousand years they had settlements along the coast, but these are only likely to have been used on a seasonal basis, probably for sealing in the autumn. People lived off the sea. Incinerated bone fragments on settlement sites suggest that fish, seal and seabirds were important items on the menu. For the remainder of the year people lived further inland and lived by hunting elk and beaver and fishing in the lakes.

Överveda has a Stone Age settlement site which was inhabited roughly between 3500 and 2500 BC. At that time it was thoroughly sheltered at the landward end of a deep bay with direct access to the archipelago outside. Today the remains of the settlement are about 70 metres above sea level and look out over undulating farmland.

The Bronze Age inhabitants of Höga Kusten appear to have lived more permanently along the coast, and they built impressive funeral monuments to their dead. The 700 or more burial cairns are strung out along what was then the coastline but is now 30 or 50 metres above sea level. They were all positioned so as to be clearly visible out to sea, and perhaps they also served as territorial markings. The settlements, though, were some distance away from the burial cairns, in sheltered bays. During the Late Bronze Age, c. 800-500 BC, people had grad-

ually begun tilling the soil and herding cattle, but the economy was still principally based on hunting and fishing.

With the Iron Age, agriculture came to Höga Kusten in earnest. Small, isolated homesteads surrounded by great tracts of forest lay scattered throughout the valleys everywhere in the region. Traces have been found, for example, of the northernmost Iron Age homestead anywhere in Sweden, Gene Fornby. Sturdy, spacious longhouses were shared by human beings and livestock, and the dead were buried in mounds close by.

Cattle-herding and barley-growing were now the main occupations, but fishing and sealing continued. Nothing, of course, could be allowed to go to waste, added to

which later on, both Church and Crown preferred taxes to be paid in train oil, hides and sealskin.

But the old trapping culture was not quite extinct. The agrarian population coexisted with hunter-gatherers who built their huts along the shoreline. The Iron Age shingle fields contain numerous traces of primitive house foundations. These date mostly from about 400 AD, but new ones were still being added until the 14th century.

Fifty metres to go

Eventually the clustered huts of the hunter-gatherers gave way to small fishing camps. Fishing has always been a major economic activity along Höga Kusten, and from medieval times until the beginning of the 20th century it was the population's paramount livelihood. All along the coast there were harbours which also served as trading points. This was very much due to the Gävle Fishermen, who moved up here for the fishing season, renting cottages from the local population at twenty or more fishing camps. During the winter season these places were often completely deserted. One of the best-known of them was Bönhamn, which today is a popular tourist attraction. Bönhamn remains a harbour, whereas Sandviken, not so very far away, was abandoned long ago and is now situated inland. Every fishing camp had a small chapel which became a natural gathering point. The oldest fishermen's chapel in the north of Sweden,

dating from 1622, is at Ulvöhamn on the island of Ulvön. Nowadays you need only say *surströmming* (fermented Baltic herring) and most people will think of Ulvön, but in the 16th century it was a centre for fishermen from

Left page, top picture: Outside the Skuleskogen national park are the small islands, Ternättholmarna, which at some time in the future may become part of the mainland. Scientists estimate that the land will rise another fifty metres or so before the effects of the ice cap have been eliminated. But that is going to take something like 10,000 years to accomplish.

Left page, bottom picture: Trysunda fishing port, outside Örnsköldsvik, is still by the shore, unlike many older fishing harbours along the High Coast.

Right: The majestic Skuleberget mountain dominates the surrounding country.

far and wide, one of the most important places anywhere on the coast.

In the 18th century the local inhabitants took over the harbours and fishing camps, which now became year-round settlements. A new heyday followed, lasting until as recently as the 1950s. Then, in the 1960s, the coastal region changed character and most of the old fishing camps were turned into holiday villages.

What of the future? Scientists expect the Höga Kusten land level to rise by another fifty metres or so in the next 10,000 years. The present-day coastal communities will find themselves a long way inland, and cobs and skerries will change into islands and peninsulas. Quite certainly, though, Höga Kusten will continue to capture scientific interest and everyone's imagination.

Above: The fragile Calypso orchid thrives in marshy woodlands and in Sweden grows from Medelpad northwards.
Below: Veda Lake, with till-capped hills in the background.

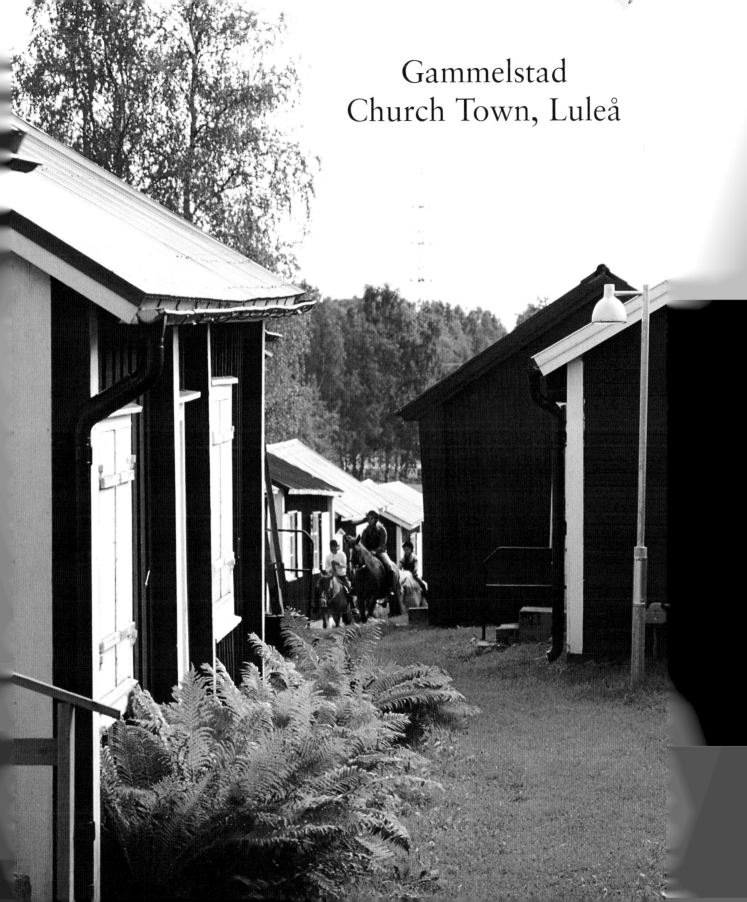

Gammelstad
Church Town, Luleå

"All farmers have their cabins by the church, in a place they call Bärghet, with two, three, four or five of them to a cabin. They arrive there every Saturday for evensong, leaving again on the Sunday evening or the Monday."

This is how Johannes Bureus, Sweden's first Keeper of National Antiquities, described Gammelstad after a visit there at Christmas 1600, and it is the first recorded mention of "church cabins". The description still holds good today. Up on a hill stands the largest medieval church in Norrland, with 425 small red-painted cabins outside the churchyard wall, lining the streets which radiate from the church in all directions. A visitor to Gammelstad on a winter's day will find most of the cabins barred and bolted, sporting massive white-painted shutters, but the odd window will be showing a light, and smoke from chimneys will confirm the existence of a small permanent population.

Most of these tiny dwelling houses are located east of the church. The area adjoining Gamla Hamngatan ("Old Harbour

Street") is occupied by larger buildings and outbuildings neatly marshalled into blocks. Hamngatan was once the main street from the church and market place down to the harbour, which in Bureus' time was barely a kilometre away from the church. In the ensuing 400 years the land has risen by four metres, and Gammelstad is now a good distance away from the coast, with the latest harbour 10 km away to the southeast. Gammelstad is only about 100 km away from the Arctic Circle.

Left: Framlämningsvägen with Nederluleå Church in the distance. The "church town" was often the final link in the long chain of command from the King to people in isolated villages. Above: In these small rooms people could only sleep and eat, but they could at least go to bed behind closed doors.

Skellefteå, Öjebyn (outside Piteå) and Gammelstad are the last "church towns" in the Nordic countries to have survived intact, retaining their old custom of occasional residence. For the big annual festivals and other ecclesiastical occasions like confirmations and weddings, the place is a bustle of activity, and the 425 church cabins, totalling 550 rooms, are full to bursting point.

The origins of the town

When Bureus celebrated Christmas here in 1600, Gammelstad had about 200 cabins. Their use can be traced back to the 16th century, but the history of both church and site goes back further still. The first written mention of Luleå comes in 1327, but this was already a trade centre in the Viking era.

walls with paintings. The church interior from the chancel screen to the organ loft is distinctly 18th century. The pulpit is decorated with gilding and bright colours. The churchyard gates, which by the look of them could have come from a castle, betoken the refuge that the church and the churchyard wall could offer in troubled times. From time to time near the end of the Middle Ages, commercial prosperity also attracted the attentions of Baltic pirates.

Kyrkberget ("Church Hill") in Gammelstad began as an islet in the archipelago, at the point of intersection between the shipping lane from the inland, the coastal shipping route from the south and the sea route across to Finland and Russia – a strategic location indeed for trading activity. As the land level rose, Gammelstad merged with the mainland. Luleå was founded to give the Swedish state control of the vast northern territories and of trade in fish (salmon mostly), furs and other commodities. Rapid population growth in Europe was creating a huge market for dried and salted fish.

Nederluleå Church – "the Cathedral of the Bothnian Gulf" – was built in the 15th century as a parish church for three river valleys and their coastal areas. In area the parish exceeded the present-day Benelux countries. It had a population of between two and three thousand. Some of the foremost craftsmen in the country came here to construct vaulting and to adorn roofs and

The "church town"

The Reformation and royal supremacy in the Nordic countries spelled compulsory church attendance. The far-flung territories of the north were thinly populated. Churches were few in number, but the people were compelled to gather for services and sermons in the parish church at fixed times during the year, and so those for whom this meant a long journey built overnight cabins near the churches. These cabins grew steadily more numerous, eventually growing into complete "church towns", not only in Sweden but in Finland and North Norway too.

The "church towns" were important meeting points where people gathered from near and far to swap news and commodities. New acquaintances were made, chil-

Right: On a winter's day nearly all the cottages are closed. Non-locals are intrigued by the sight of an entire town apparently in mothballs.
Below: Even the houses which are only used very occasionally have been carefully preserved, both inside and out.

dren were christened, couples were given in marriage and the dead were buried. Taxation rolls were drawn up and taxes collected. Public announcements were made outside the church, and this too was where the young men of the parish were enrolled for military service. The "church town" goings-on were not always in harmony with the precepts of the Church and the letter of the scriptures. Church festivals were, not least, a welcome change from the brow-sweating business of toiling for one's daily bread.

Round about the Gammelstad "church town" there

eventually sprang up a perfectly ordinary town with all the important community functions this implies. Luleå received its charter in 1621. Community matters and trade were to be conducted in an orderly fashion. By tradition, the different village communities had built cabins along the approach roads to the church. The area east of the church was now cleared and parcelled out into regular plots on which the townspeople built houses lining the main street leading down to the harbour.

But the harbour had grown too shallow – not, as people then believed, due to the Baltic losing water, but because the land had been steadily rising ever since the last glacial. In 1649 the town was transferred to the present harbour, 10 km further southeast. Many people stayed on in the old town, and Luleå was divided into Lule Nystad (New Town) and Lule Gammelstad (Old Town). Gammelstad became both town and "church town", a place with both a permanent and a seasonal population.

Gammelstad in recent times

A new age came to Lule Nystad, while Gammelstad lapsed into obscurity. Gammelstad remained, however, a meeting point for parishioners arriving on their regular visits.

The religious revival movements spread through part of the Nordic countries like wildfire during the 19th century. The old tavern opposite Gammelstad Church was cleansed of its sinful past and took on a new lease of life as the Bethel chapel. In many places the "church towns" gradually ceased to be used. Better communications and the growth of population led to a subdivision of the old parishes. The social influence of the Church steadily diminished during the 20th century. There can be no doubt that the custom of church festivals in Gammelstad has continued to flourish down to our own times because the "church town" serves as much of a social as a religious purpose. The use of the church cabins is still governed by statutes applying to all participants.

Gammelstad has become a time capsule and embodies the changing conditions and life styles of many centuries. It can be experienced as a lovely idyll, but it is very much a monument to the conditions which people were forced to adapt to. Gammelstad is still a living environment. Parishioners still come here for church festivals, just as generation upon generation has done before them.

Previous spread: View from the church tower, looking south-west. Below: Rutviksvägen. The towered building houses the World Heritage office for Gammelstad Church Town.

Laponia

From the primitive forests and wetlands of Muddus and Stubba in the lowlands the landscape rises to the undulating forests and mountains of Sjaunja. The Stora Sjöfallet national park is located to either side of Lake Akkajaure. Southwards the terrain rises to Alpine mountains in Sarek and undulating mountain meadows in Padjelanta. Sulitema, at the western extreme, with its great glaciers and tall peaks, forms the border with Norway.

Glaciers and valleys traverse the landscape, apparently unchangeable and unaffected by human activity and interference. In Sarek, the national park in the heart of Lapland, steep, massive mountain peaks soar heavenwards.

Sweden acquired its first national parks in 1909, when Sarek and Stora Sjöfallet were thus designated together with seven other areas. Today these two national parks are a part of the Lapland World Heritage site, Laponia, which also includes another two national parks – Padjelanta and Muddus – and two nature reserves – Stubba and Sjaunja. Together they total 9,400 km². Laponia extends 200 km from east to west and 80 km from north to south. Lengthwise, from the Norwegian border to Porjus, it is divided by lakes Akkajaure and Stora Lulevatten.

Ancient man-made landscape

The Laponia World Heritage site is one of the last great wildernesses of Western Europe – a great expanse of flora and fauna, undisturbed by modern society. This is wild and trackless country of high mountains, open mountain plateaux, endless forests and far-flung wetlands. The fauna includes brown bear, wolverine, lynx and large elk which develop enormous shovel antlers. There is an abundance of birdlife, with gyrfalcon, golden eagle and white-tailed eagle hunting in the mountain valleys. In summer the wetlands and watercourses are abuzz with mosquitoes and a myriad of other insects.

Man has lived off this country from time immemorial. The mountain valleys, primitive forests and river banks are a vital necessity to the reindeer. The oldest traces of human settlement date back 9,000 years. Both landscape and climate have changed during that time, and man has adapted to new conditions. Hunting of wild

Page 127: Kungsleden at Aktse. In the distance, the sharp profile of Skierffe Mountain pierces the skyline.
Left: A moss-clad grindstone at what used to be the new settlement of Aktse, below Skierffe.
Above: Boat on the shore of Lake Sádishávrre.

reindeer was followed by domestication and herding. Water and ice continue to shape the landscape, in a process which has been going on since the last glacial.

Basically, Laponia consists of two entirely different sorts of landscape. The eastern part is plainland, with extensive wetlands, forests and lakes. About 100,000 hectares of this are conifer forest, in which the oldest living pine trees have stood for over 700 years. Here too are the largest wetlands in the Nordic area. Forest and wetlands form large areas of mosaic. Scattered hills and low mountains punctuate the plainland, especially to the westward, where the landscape rises towards the high mountains.

Left: The Sarek national park, in the heart of Laponia, includes the last European wilderness, with steep mountains, great glaciers, deep valleys and fast-flowing rivers. Visible in the background is the Akka massif.
Right: Hikers at Darreluoppal on the Padjelanta Trail.
Below: Stora Sjöfallet, between lakes Kårtjejaure and Langas, has a total drop of 40 metres. It consists of several separate watercourses plunging over a number of cliff ledges. The flow of water was dramatically reduced by the regulation of the Suorva dam in 1922.

The west has the other type of Laponian landscape – variegated mountain scenery. The Sarek and Stora Sjöfallet national parks include deep valleys and untamed rivers in between steep, pointed mountains. Sarek alone numbers 200 mountain peaks, more than half of them over 1,800 metres high. Sarek also has about 100 glaciers. The deeply gouged Rapadalen is one of the most impressive mountain valleys in Scandinavia. In Padjelanta national park, west of Sarek, the mountain landscape changes to vast levels and great lakes. The copious flora includes more than 400 vascular plant species.

Geology

The mountains of Padjelanta and Sarek were created more than 420 million years ago, when Scandinavia and North America collided. The Appalachians arose in North America, and the Scandinavian mountain range was formed on the other side of the Atlantic.

The bedrock of the different parts of Laponia is extremely varied. Padjelanta, the mountain expanses to the west, originated as gravel and clay on the seabed. These sediments solidified into porous rocks. With the passing of time they have been worn down into the relatively low and rounded formations we see today. The dark, high, steep mountains of Sarek consist of a harder, volcanic rock, amphibolite.

The refashioning of the landscape during the glacials is especially conspicuous. Distinct traces of the retreating ice cap are visible on the bare mountain. Gravel and pebbles from the mountain sides were carried along by the meltwater. The material thus detached was deposited in deep spots and along the watercourses. In this way the landscape as we see it today is the product of several ice ages.

When the climate turned colder, about 100,000 years ago, glaciers formed on the high mountains, expanding towards low-lying areas until eventually the greater part of Northern Europe was covered by them – in the last Ice Age, with only the very highest mountain peaks protruding. With the return of warmer times, 10,000 years ago, the ice cap retreated. The weight and movements of the ice gouged narrow V-shaped clefts into open U-shaped valleys. The deep ravines of Stora Sjöfallet and southern Muddus originated as small fissures in the rock which were expanded by the meltwater from the ice cap. Heavy deposits of gravel and sand – glacial till – were left behind.

Five thousand years ago, Sweden was free from ice, except for the glaciers in the north, but the landscape is still changing. The frost breaks away boulders of various sizes which lie in huge quantities along the mountain sides of Sarek, and the ground frost moves both earth and stone. Ice erosion and meltwater are breaking down the mountains, and the water carries with it sand and gravel, just as it has been doing ever since the great ice cap melted.

The Scandinavian mountain range is unique in that the tree line is marked by broadleaf trees – primarily mountain birch, but also including the pussy willow.

The weather in these mountain regions is highly changeable. The Laponia climate varies with distance from and height above the sea. The high mountains in the west have unstable weather conditions, with low pressure areas and precipitation sweeping in from the Atlantic. The summers are cool and short. Further east in the forest country, a more stable, inland climate prevails, the summers are warmer and the annual precipitation less copious.

The man-made landscape

When the ice released its hold and flora and fauna returned, man was able to live by fishing and by hunting. Laponia has been continuously inhabited for 9,000 years. Stone Age tools that old have been found at Kåretjaure in the Stora Sjöfallet national park.

The Sami (Lapps) are the indigenous population of the Arctic region. From prehistoric times they have lived in the region comprising the Kola Peninsula and the northernmost parts of Finland, Norway and Sweden. Archaeological finds have shown that from about 1000 BC onwards two distinct cultural traditions came into being in this region. The design of bronze and, subsequently, iron objects indicates membership of a general Western and Central European civilisation on the one hand, and on the other a culture subject to eastern influence.

Ever since prehistoric times, the Sami settlements have been divided into regions, vuobme. Every region in turn was divided into smaller areas, siida. The siida was both a group of people and a geographic area. Settlements were adapted to the seasons of the year. The hut in the pictures above is situated at an old Sami camp at Duolbuk, or Tuolpuk, in the municipality of Jokkmokk.
Next spread: This Sami summer camp is still in use. It is at Vastenjaure, or Vastenjávrre, in the municipality of Jokkmokk.

The traces left by people in past ages are very discreet, almost invisible, but they are there. Visitors expecting to see virgin scenery can suddenly stumble on a stone cairn surrounding a pit. There are thousands of these ancient trapping pits scattered throughout the terrain, carefully constructed at a time when the wild reindeer were an important part of man's livelihood. They bear witness to systematic, organised hunting along the game animals' migration paths. A long-deserted settlement site can be betrayed by unusually lush vegetation and the remains of hearths and storage cellars dug into the earth. Promontories and isles may hold well-concealed burial places from pre-Christian times. Votive sites are often marked with stones or wooden figures, but can equally well be associated with peculiar natural formations invested with mystical, religious significance.

Settlement was periodic and followed the pattern of the seasons, which, in Sami tradition, were eight in number. The winter settlements were usually in the forest country beside large watercourses with opportunities for hunting and fishing. In the spring people migrated to settlements in the border country between forest and mountain. In summertime they lived beside big rivers in the exposed mountain areas, where everyone took part in

Left: The Stalo Stone, an ancient place of sacrifice, is a very discreet archaeological site. In the terrain round about, the trained eye can spot other traces of earlier habitation.
Below: The reindeer has been the companion of the Sami for thousands of years. This one met its fate at Vastenjaure.
Right: The Chapel at Alkavare, Álggavárre in Sami, is the most isolated in Sweden.

fishing, fowling and the gathering of plants and berries. They followed the migration of the reindeer flock, moving from one settlement to another.

Traces of settlements are still visible, mostly as rectangular stone settings, hearths. The so-called *stalo* sites may have been foundations for huts above the tree line. They usually occur in two or three lines.

The Sami domesticated the reindeer sometime during the first century of the Christian era, working it as a draught and pack animal and using its meat, innards, hide, horns and bones. Specialisation in reindeer herding made new demands on settlement and migration. The reindeer herds needed access to pasture and had to be watched over.

The reindeer herds became individual property, which meant the herdsmen rounding up their reindeer and migrating with them between different grazing areas. The reindeer owners formed Sami villages. A Sami village *(sameby)* is an economic and administrative association, but also a geographic area in which the members run their herds together. Laponia today has six mountain Sami villages and a forest Sami village.

Present and future

The past hundred years have wrought great changes on the landscape, flora and fauna of northern Sweden. Roads and railways have been constructed for new mining communities, and hydropower, not least, has left its mark on the rivers. The Luleälven river, with sources within the World Heritage site, is one of the most thoroughly harnessed of all. The biggest reservoirs are pent-up lakes dividing the Stora Sjöfallet national park in two. Modern forestry, with its clear-felling and replanting methods, has changed the vegetation and fauna, but the primitive forest and wetlands of Laponia still include biotopes and biodiversity which used to extend over greater areas.

Laponia is a magnificent wilderness with majestic primeval forests, unspoiled wetlands, high mountains and delta areas of outstanding natural beauty. This is a dynamic landscape in which can be observed the ongoing transforming power of natural forces. People have lived and worked here for thousands of years. This is a living landscape, with a lifestyle dominated by man's interaction with nature.

Nature will not be halted, as witness this ancient pine tree growing at Satis, Sádis in Sami. The oldest of living pine trees within the World Heritage site are more than 700 years old, and huge areas are covered by mosaics of primitive forest and wetlands. But human beings have also gained a foothold in this grim world, ever since the ice cap released its hold, 10,000 years ago.

Facts and Inscription Criteria in Brief

THE NAVAL PORT OF KARLSKRONA

Karlskrona in Blekinge, founded in 1680, was one of the most modern and most efficient naval bases of the time. The shipyard, architecture, urban planning, and the way in which installations and defences were constructed aroused attention throughout Europe in the 18th century. Karlskrona's naval heritage has been continued down to our own times, with over 300 years' unbroken activity in the naval base and the shipyard.

The Naval Port of Karlskrona was inscribed on the World Heritage List in 1998.

Part of the World Heritage Committee's citation reads: *Karlskrona is an exceptionally well preserved example of a European planned naval town, which incorporates elements derived from earlier establishments in other countries and which was in its turn to serve as the model for subsequent towns with similar functions. Naval bases played an important role in the centuries during which naval power was a determining factor in European Realpolitik, and Karlskrona is the best preserved and most complete of those that survive.*

THE AGRICULTURAL LANDSCAPE OF SOUTHERN ÖLAND

This World Heritage site, comprising upwards of 56,000 hectares, includes arable land, grazing land, villages, prehistoric forts and expanses of water. Man has been using the terrain here for several millennia, creating a unique man-made and natural landscape bearing multiple traces of different periods of history and prehistory, side by side with a living agrarian community.

The agricultural landscape of Southern Öland was inscribed on the World Heritage List in 2000.

Part of the World Heritage Committee's citation reads: *The landscape of Southern Öland takes its contemporary form from its long cultural history, adapting to the physical constraints of the geology and topography. Southern Öland is an outstanding example of human settlement, making the optimum use of diverse landscape types on a single island.*

THE HANSEATIC TOWN OF VISBY

Visby, on the west coast of Gotland, is one of the most popular destinations for summer tourism. But it is also a remarkable combination of an idyllic, hundred-year-old small town and a big medieval town. It is a typical Hanseatic town with an encircling wall, a well-preserved street grid, and buildings from the Middle Ages onwards. Medieval church ruins and warehouses blend with the low houses of wood and stone from later periods.

The Hanseatic town of Visby was inscribed on the World Heritage List in 1995.

Part of the World Heritage Committee's citation reads:
Visby is an outstanding example of a Northern European walled Hanseatic town which has in a unique way preserved its townscape and its extremely valuable buildings, which in form and function clearly reflect this significant human settlement.

THE ROCK CARVINGS IN TANUM

The rock carvings in Tanum, in the north of Bohuslän, transport the visitor back to the social and religious life of the Bronze Age. The Tanum site contains more than 350 greatly varied groups of carvings, extending over the smooth-worn rock faces. They are construed as early symbolic pictorial art, the themes and positioning of which were carefully planned by their creators.

The Tanum prehistoric rock carvings were inscribed on the World Heritage List in 1994.

Part of the World Heritage Committee's citation reads:
The rock carvings in the Tanum area are unique examples of Bronze Age art of the highest quality. The range of motifs provides rare evidence of many aspects of life in the European Bronze Age. The landscape in Tanum testifies to uninterrupted settlement in the area, covering over eight thousand years of human history.

Skogskyrkogården – The Woodland cemetery

The Skogskyrkogården cemetery in Enskede, southern Stockholm, was built between 1919 and 1940 by the architects Gunnar Asplund and Sigurd Lewerentz. On a ridge overgrown with pines they created a sacred landscape with several small chapels arranged to interact with the natural surroundings. The entire site is considered one of the most important works of modern architecture.

Skogskyrkogården was inscribed on the World Heritage List in 1994.

Part of the World Heritage Committee's citation reads:
Skogskyrkogården is an outstanding example of how architecture and landscaping from our century combine to make a cemetery. This creation has had a great influence on the design of cemeteries all over the world.

The Royal Domain of Drottningholm

The Royal Domain of Drottningholm on the island of Lovön, Stockholm, was the first Swedish site on the World Heritage List. The crucial factor for the decision by the World Heritage Committee was the presence of two special buildings in the domain: the Chinese Pavilion and the Drottningholm Palace Theatre. Drottningholm Palace, a listed historic building, is now the residence of the royal family. The park, the Chinese Pavilion, and the Drottningholm Palace Theatre are open to the public.

The Royal Domain of Drottningholm was inscribed on the World Heritage List in 1991.

Part of the World Heritage Committee's citation reads:
The Drottningholm site – the palace, the theatre, the Chinese Pavilion, and the park – is the best example in Sweden of a royal 18th century residence, representative of all European architecture from this period. Drottningholm Palace was influenced by the French king's Versailles, as were many other palaces in Europe at this time.

Birka and Hovgården

During the Viking era, Birka, on the island of Björkö in Lake Mälaren, was the economic hub of the prosperous Mälaren valley. The town, established in the 8th century, became an important centre of trade and an international port for visitors from near and far. Hovgården, on the island of Adelsö, opposite, has unusually copious traces of the royalty, magnates and farmers of the Viking era.

The Birka-Hovgården area was inscribed on the World Heritage List in 1993.

Part of the World Heritage Committee's citation reads:

The Birka-Hovgården area is a well preserved example of the Vikings' trading networks during the two centuries when they expanded economically and politically in Europe. Birka is one of the most complete and untouched Viking Age trading sites from the years 700-900.

The Engelsberg Ironworks

Engelsberg Ironworks in Västmanland was constructed in 1681 and developed into one of the world's most modern ironworks in the period 1700-1800. The site comprises the mansion and park, works offices, workers' homes, and industrial buildings. Engelsberg is the only ironworks in Sweden that still preserves the buildings and most of the technical equipment.

Engelsberg was inscribed on the World Heritage List in 1993.

Part of the World Heritage Committee's citation reads:
Engelsberg is an outstanding example of an important European industry from the 17th to the 19th centuries, with important technical remains and with both offices and homes preserved.

THE MINING AREA OF THE GREAT COPPER MOUNTAIN IN FALUN

The shiny red metal from the Falun copper mine was shipped out to be made into roofs for cathedrals and palaces all over Europe. Today the Great Copper Mountain (Stora Kopparberget) and the surrounding landscape are a unique memento of Sweden's early history as an industrial nation.

Stora Kopparberget and Falun were inscribed on the World Heritage List in 2001.

Part of the World Heritage Committee's citation reads:
The historic industrial landscape surrounding the Great Copper Mountain and Falun is one of the foremost areas associated with mining and metal production. Mining operations were discontinued at the close of the 20th century, but for many centuries they exerted a powerful influence on technical, economic, social and political developments in Sweden and Europe.

HÖGA KUSTEN – THE HIGH COAST

Nowhere else in the world has post-glacial isostatic uplift been so great as on the High Coast. After the ice had melted, 9,600 years ago, a new land rose from the sea and was successively colonised by flora and fauna. Humans settled here, leaving their mark on the beautiful, distinctive landscape, with its sweeping mountain contours, steep cliffs plunging vertically down to the sea and coves and inlets winding their way in between the islands.

The High Coast was inscribed on the World Heritage List in 2000.

Part of the World Heritage Committee's citation reads:
The site is one of the places in the world that is experiencing isostatic uplift as a result of deglaciation. Isostatic rebound is well-illustrated and the distinctiveness of the site is the extent of the total isostatic uplift which, at 285 m, exceeds others. The site is the "type area" for research on isostacy, the phenomenon having been first recognised and studied there.

Gammelstad Church Town

Gammelstad in Luleå is the largest preserved church town in northern Norrland. It is moreover the only one which combines the two types of wooden towns in Scandinavia – the church town and the borough. A church town is a group of houses and stables used by parishioners who lived far away from the church. They stayed here during the big church holidays, courts, markets, and other occasions.

Gammelstad Church Town was inscribed on the World Heritage List in 1996.

Part of the World Heritage Committee's citation reads:
Gammelstad Church Town is a unique example of the traditional church town found in northern Scandinavia. It illustrates in an outstanding way the adaptation of traditional town planning to the distinctive geographical and climatological conditions prevailing in a difficult natural environment.

Laponia

The Laponian area is Europe's largest continuous area of virtually untouched nature. It has steep mountain massifs and extensive mountain plains, glaciers, wetlands, and primeval forests, torrential waterfalls and large mountain lakes. In addition, it has a rich animal and plant life, with several endangered species.

Laponia was inscribed on the World Heritage List in 1996.

Part of the World Heritage Committee's citation concerning the natural qualities of the site reads:
The area is an outstanding example of how the earth has developed, especially geologically, and how ecological and biological changes happen today. There are also unique natural phenomena of exceptional natural beauty and significant natural localities for the protection of biological diversity.

As regards the cultural qualities of the site, part of the citation reads:
The Laponian cultural heritage in northern Sweden, which has been inhabited by the Sami since prehistoric times, is one of the best preserved examples of a nomadic area in northern Scandinavia. It contains settlements and pastures for large herds of reindeer, a custom that was once very common, going back to an early stage in human economic and social development.